Library of
Davidson College

*A
New Look at
Portfolio Management*

**CONTEMPORARY STUDIES IN
ECONOMIC AND FINANCIAL ANALYSIS VOL. V**

Editors: Professor Edward I. Altman and Ingo Walter, Associate Dean
School of Business Administration, New York University

CONTEMPORARY STUDIES IN ECONOMIC AND FINANCIAL ANALYSIS

An International Series of Monographs

Series Editors: Edward I. Altman and Ingo Walter
Graduate School of Business Administration, New York University

Volume 1. DYNAMICS OF FORECASTING FINANCIAL CYCLES: THEORY, TECHNIQUE AND IMPLEMENTATION
Lacy H. Hunt, *Fidelcor, Inc. and the Fidelity Bank*

Volume 2. COMPOSITE RESERVE ASSETS IN THE INTERNATIONAL MONETARY SYSTEM
Jacob S. Dreyer, *Graduate School of Arts and Science, New York University*

Volume 3. APPLICATION OF CLASSIFICATION TECHNIQUES IN BUSINESS, BANKING AND FINANCE
Edward I. Altman, *Graduate School of Business Administration, New York University;* Robert B. Avery, *Graduate School of Industrial Administration, Carnegie-Mellon University;* Robert A. Eisenbeis and Joseph F. Sinkey, Jr., *both Federal Deposit Insurance Corporation*

Volume 4. PROBLEM AND FAILED INSTITUTIONS IN THE COMMERCIAL BANKING INDUSTRY
Joseph F. Sinkey, Jr., *Federal Deposit Insurance Corporation*

Volume 5. A NEW LOOK AT PORTFOLIO MANAGEMENT
David M. Ahlers, *Graduate School of Business and Public Administration, Cornell University*

Volume 6. MULTINATIONAL ELECTRONIC COMPANIES AND NATIONAL ECONOMIC POLICIES
Edmond Sciberras, *Science Policy Research Unit, University of Sussex*

Volume 7. VENEZUELAN ECONOMIC DEVELOPMENT: A POLITICO-ECONOMIC ANALYSIS
Loring Allen, *University of Missouri, St. Louis*

Volume 8. ENVIRONMENT, PLANNING AND THE MULTINATIONAL CORPORATION
Thomas N. Gladwin, *Centre d'Etudes Industrielles and New York University*

Volume 9. FOREIGN DIRECT INVESTMENT, INDUSTRIALIZATION AND SOCIAL CHANGE
Stephen J. Kobrin, *Alfred P. Sloan School of Management, Massachusetts Institute of Technology*

Volume 10. IMPLICATIONS OF REGULATION ON BANK EXPANSION: A SIMULATION ANALYSIS
George Oldfield, Jr., *The Amos Tuck School of Business Adminstration, Dartmouth College*

Volume 11.   IMPORT SUBSTITUTION, TRADE AND DEVELOPMENT
Jaleel Ahmad, *Concordia University, Sir George Williams Campus*

Volume 12.   CORPORATE GROWTH AND COMMON STOCK RISK
David Fewings, *McGill University*

Volume 13.   CAPITAL MARKET EQUILIBRIUM AND CORPORATE FINANCIAL DECISIONS
Richard C. Stapleton, *Manchester Business School, England and New York University* and M.G. Subrahmanyam, *Indian Institute of Management, Ahmedbad and New York University*

Volume 14.   IMPENDING CHANGES FOR SECURITIES MARKETS: WHAT ROLE FOR THE EXCHANGES?
Ernest Bloch and Robert A. Schwartz, *Graduate School of Business Administration, New York University*

Volume 15.   INDUSTRIAL INNOVATION AND INTERNATIONAL TRADING PERFORMANCE
William B. Walker, *Science Policy Research Unit, University of Sussex*

Volume 16.   FINANCIAL POLICY, INFLATION AND ECONOMIC DEVELOPMENT: THE MEXICAN EXPERIENCE
John K. Thompson, *New York University*

Volume 17.   THE MANAGEMENT OF CORPORATE LIQUIDITY
Michel Levasseur, *Centre d'Enseignement Superieur des Affaires, Jouy-en-Josas, France*

Volume 18.   STABILIZATION OF INTERNATIONAL COMMODITY MARKETS
Paul Hallwood, *University of Aberdeen*

Volume 19.   PROBLEMS IN EUROPEAN CORPORATE FINANCE: TEXT AND CASES
Michel Schlosser, *Centre d'Enseignement Superieur des Affaires, Jouy-en-Josas, France*

Volume 20.   THE MULTINATIONAL ENTERPRISE: INTERNATIONAL INVESTMENT AND HOST COUNTRY IMPACTS
Thomas G. Parry, *School of Economics, University of New South Wales*

A New Look at Portfolio Management

by DAVID M. AHLERS
Graduate School of Business and Public Administration
Cornell University

Foreword by Professor KALMAN J. COHEN
Graduate School of Business Administration
Duke University

JAI PRESS
Greenwich, Connecticut

Library of Congress Cataloging in Publication Data

Ahlers, David M
  A new look at portfolio management.

  (Contemporary studies in economic and financial analysis ; v. 5)
  A revision of the author's thesis, Carnegie-Mellon University, 1975.
  Bibliography: p.
  Includes index.

  1. Investments. 2. Investment analysis. 3. Pension trusts—Investments. 4. Institutional investments. I. Title. II. Series.
  HG4539.A38   1977   332.6'7   76-10448
  ISBN 0-89232-012-5

Copyright © 1977 by JAI Press
321 Greenwich Avenue
Greenwich, Connecticut 06830
All rights reserved
ISBN: 0-89232-012-5
Library of Congress Catalog Card Number 76-10448
Manufactured in the United States of America

FOREWORD

My personal definition of *management science* is: "Management science is the application of scientific concepts and quantitative techniques to help executives in large, complex organizations solve their planning, decision-making, and control problems." In keeping with this definition, the research described in this book by Professor David M. Ahlers, *A New Look at Portfolio Management*, is an outstanding example of management science. The Structured Decision Making System developed by the author was, for several years, effectively implemented in the trust department of a major New York City bank. Hence this book describes one of those all-too-rare examples of management science models that actually were used as part of the management process, and it does not belong to the realm of "management science fiction" (proposed models that never have been implemented) that seems to fill the professional literature.

The phrase "to help executives" is one part of my definition of management science which I particularly stress. I believe that the emphasis of management science should be to help executives, rather than to replace executives by automating the management process. In order to build effective management science models that will in fact be used to help executives, a great deal of behavioral knowledge and organizational expertise is required. Also, a great deal of tact, patience, and understanding is necessary. That the author possesses and utilizes such knowledge and skill is evident from Chapter 3 of this book, where he discusses relevant organizational considerations.

For a management scientist to be able to formulate models that will be effectively utilized in the management process, he or she must have a sound understanding of management problems, the type and quality of information available to management, and the relevant institutional environment. That the author has this understanding is evident in Chapter 2 of this book, where he discusses the pension fund management environment. In both Chapters 2 and 3, the author shows that he has a thorough knowledge of the latest academic developments in areas of finance, economics, and management science and that he understands why relevent institutional, behavioral, and organizational factors have prevented what seems like "obvious good academic sense" from being applied in practice in the pension fund management area.

There is, of course, considerable scope for the right type of mathematical models and quantitative techniques to be developed to help management to improve its planning, decision-making, and control processes. That the author understands the appropriate mathematics and is skillful at model building is evident from the developments in Chapter 4 of this book. All of the many relevant approaches, together with the underlying institutional understanding, are synthesized in Chapter 5 of this book, where the author evaluates alternative decision-making systems for pension fund management. Here some of the traditional "great truths" of modern academic theory are shattered!

The conclusions developed in Chapter 6 of this book should interest portfolio managers, security analysts, management scientists, financial theorists, and people whose assets are managed by professional investment managers. A great deal of food for thought which is developed throughout the book gets highlighted in this concluding chapter.

Many academicians will find this book disquieting because it attacks some of the shibboleths of modern portfolio theory. Certainly the capital asset pricing model is a comfortable ideology, erected upon the concept of efficient markets. However, the evidence developed by the author in this research, based on actual forecasts made by security analysts in a major financial institution, indicates that there may be ways in which institutional investors can attain significantly better than random returns even after all management fees and transaction costs are considered.

Institutional investors will find this book particularly interesting, since it shows how computer-based models can be effectively used as components in the investment management process. This book presents the relevant tools and techniques. The costs of developing and implementing these models is relatively small, compared to the potential returns from doing so.

Some who read this book will find it controversial, and will look for ways to refute its claims. All who read it, however, will find it to be stimulating, provocative, thoughtful, and insightful.

Even though this research initially began as a Ph.D. thesis at Carnegie-Mellon University's Graduate School of Industrial Administration, from the beginning it was more pragmatic in orientation than are most doctoral dissertations. From the outset, the author was interested in developing security evaluation models and portfolio management models which could be used by institutional investors to improve their investment management process. He was able to obtain information and data from several major banks involved in the management of pension funds. As chairman of his doctoral dissertation committee, I was pleased with the progress that he was making and felt sure that he was close to completing a good Ph.D. thesis.

One of the reasons why doctoral dissertation chairmen get gray hairs is that their students sometimes accept full-time employment before their theses are completed. This usually causes long delays in completion of the dissertations, some students give up without ever completing them, and seldom is the quality of the theses improved by these delays. In the case of the author, soon before I thought that his dissertation could have been completed, he accepted full-time employment with a major New York City bank. As is typical, this led to a delay of several years in his thesis being completed, but happily it was finally finished, and he received his Ph.D. degree at Carnegie-Mellon University in May, 1975. This is the only case that I have seen where the quality of the dissertation was vastly improved by the several years' delay in its completion. The reason is that in his position as Director of Management Science for a large New York City bank, the author was able to broaden and deepen his knowledge of the pension fund management process, gather a unique data base that consisted of predictions of future stock prices made by security analysts, and get many of his ideas for improving the pension fund management process effectively implemented. Had the author completed his Ph.D. dissertation before starting to work full time, his thesis would have been a good one. As it developed, it became an outstanding dissertation which, after some revisions, has become the manuscript for this book.

I personally have enjoyed reading this book many times (in various phases of its development, as well as in its finished form). I enthusiastically recommend it to you.

KALMAN J. COHEN
Distinguished Bank Research Professor
Graduate School of Business Administration
Duke University
Durham, North Carolina

Preface

This book concerns the workings of the portfolio management process. Unlike most academic and professional literature of investments, this book does not propose a better way to analyze corporate financial statements or to forecast market movements. It assumes that the reader has read the appropriate material and is doing the best he can in these fundamental activities. Instead, this book addresses the problem of making the best decisions possible with the information at hand. Although potentially valuable for the single investor, it is really intended for the manager of a portfolio management department in a bank, insurance firm, brokerage firm, mutual fund or corporation. It should also prove valuable to the business or economics educator who is anxious to make his students aware of the limitations of current investment theory and the practical realities of the money management world.

Ten years ago as a student at Carnegie Institute of Technology, I began work on a Ph.D. dissertation which was to specify the steps necessary to automate the pension fund management process. Day-to-day work on this dissertation was interrupted, however, when I accepted a position as director of management science for a large New York City bank. Prior to taking this position I had developed and tested in another large bank an equity valuation model. This model, when subjected to simulation tests, was significantly superior to security analysts in the bank in its ability to select buys, and generally better in its ability to predict sales. As a by-product of this research, I had also written a computer language, IAL [5], which was intended to enable security analysts to construct their own earnings and price forecasting systems. With this background, I fully expected to complete quickly the final portion to link equity valuation models into a portfolio management system.

Upon arrival at the New York City bank I learned that they had independently constructed their own equity valuation model with similar positive results, but that it was not being used. From the new vantage point as a manager, I soon discovered that even though equity valuation models might generate better buy or sell decisions than security analysts, even when evaluated by the same criteria, the decision-making structure of the bank precluded the acceptance of any equity valuation or portfolio management models. Professional colleagues and other institutional investors, rejoined that their experiences and conclusions were very similar to mine. Fortunately, the management of our Trust Department concurred with us that computer models alone, even if they appeared to work, were of little value. Then began an effort to restructure our investment decision-making process to at least make it amendable to new equity valuation and portfolio management procedures.

During this entire period, the management of the Trust Department of the Bank, my staff and even our customers had faith that better ways of making decisions would necessarily generate better investment results. The Bank reported interim progress in its annual reports and my colleagues and I presented our findings to both the academic and professional communities [8] [9]. This phase of the research is presented in Chapter 3.

This experience altered my original research goals, set six years earlier, in three major ways. *One*, it was decided to examine the role of portfolio management models in a real-world institutional context. Models, for example, cannot be responsible for decisions to Trustees. Nor can they present testimony in Prudent Man suits. On the other hand, a model may be theoretically valid overall, but inconsistent with the individual goals and responsibilities of the people who make up the organization. Earlier research aims had been limited to a mathematical integration of theoretical equity valuation and portfolio management models. *Secondly*, I had not planned to test my combined equity valuation and portfolio management system beyond comparing its performance with the results obtained by using just the equity valuation model and a simple equal dollar investment strategy. In this study, the role of a portfolio management model has been changed. Instead of being the main result, it is now the tool used to simulate and to evaluate alternative investment decision-making systems. Although this study does present a new intertemporal portfolio management algorithm which incorporates, for example, transaction costs, management fees and feedback correction, the emphasis is managerial. Finally, in earlier research I had planned to use forecasts from computer models of stock price formulation to generate inputs to the portfolio management model. However, as a byproduct of work at the bank, the tests in this study are based on probability distributions for the prices of over 200 common stocks supplied by security analysts on a monthly basis over a two-year period. These forecasts formed the basis for the official investment policy of the bank during this time and as such, represent the forecasts behind management decisions on 13.7 percent of all pension funds managed by banks. The conclusions reached in this study are directly applicable to this bank and, based on the general management problems discussed in Chapters 2 and 3, very relevant to other investment management firms as well. In summary, the focus of my research has evolved from the specification of portfolio management tools to an examination of specific hypotheses about the portfolio management process itself.

> What form should hypotheses about the portfolio management process take? At the most fundamental level, for example, one might ask, IS investment performance actually improved by a new management system?

Testing this and related hypotheses is complicated by the fact that it was difficult enough to convince management to install one new money management system, let alone several systems simultaneously to permit controlled tests. Consequently, a general intertemporal portfolio management model with transaction costs, management fees and feedback correction was constructed to simulate portfolio management decisions over varying management information systems and varying management goals. In Chapters 5 and 6 the discussion turns to the results of these tests, and the implications for management of the following questions:

1. Does market efficiency dominate any potential benefits from a portfolio management system beyond risk-return balancing? In short, can analysts, after risk adjustments, pick enough winners over losers to justify the expense of the effort?

2. Do portfolios constructed according to classic portfolio theory significantly outperform the risk-adjusted single stock selection methods used by most institutional investors?

3. How much performance, if any, does an institution give up by using qualitative ranking systems, e.g. favorable plus, etc., instead of quantitative, probabilistic measures?

4. How sensitive are decisions to changes in the level of risk, selection of performance measures, the analysts ability to estimate changing relationships in the market?

5. Should analysts and managers be paid according to their performance as measured by comprehensive feedback evaluation systems?

Any research effort which spans a number of years, as this one has, incurs many intellectual and emotional debts to professional acquaintances, friends and family. It is, therefore, not with risk, but with certainty of committing many errors of omission, that I express my gratitude.

My overriding obligation is to Professor Kalman J. Cohen. Without his faith and insistence that I would some day complete my dissertation, I am certain I would never have done so. The support of the Ford Foundation for three years was critical in helping me to complete my studies at Carnegie-Mellon's Graduate School of Industrial Administration.

All of the research in this book was done during my employment by a large New York City bank and, recently, by the Graduate School of Business and Public Administration at Cornell University. I am grateful for their cooperation in permitting me to include this research as much as possible in my normal duties.

I am deeply indebted to Marc Steglitz for his early work with me in trying to structure the nature of the institutional problem and for his subsequent efforts, along with those of Allan Martin, in implementing the Structured Decision-Making System presented in Chapter 3. Without their efforts combined with the work performed by Martha Ferry and Jeffrey Smith, there would have been no subjective data base for this study.

My greatest professional debt, however, is to the many security analysts, portfolio managers and bank executives, who, in spite of many valid and concrete reasons to the contrary, were willing to make a daily commitment to improving their own decision-making processes.

Finally, both the encouragement provided and the sacrifices endured by my family supplied the final push needed to make me return from the business world to academia to complete this book.

DAVID M. AHLERS

CONTENTS

Foreword vii
Preface xi

I Introduction
PURPOSE 3
METHODOLOGY 4
SCOPE 10

II Pension Fund Management Environment
SIZE AND CONCENTRATION 12
INVESTMENT POLICY 13
PEOPLE IN PENSION FUND MANAGEMENT 15
EXTERNAL PRESSURES FOR CHANGE 17

III Organizational Analysis
FORMAL ORGANIZATION 26
FUNCTIONAL ORGANIZATION 30
BEHAVIORAL ANALYSIS 37
OFF-THE-SHELF MANAGEMENT SCIENCE 43
STRUCTURED DECISION MAKING 51
SDM AND ORGANIZATIONAL CHANGE 66

IV A General Pension Fund Management Simulator

OVERVIEW OF REPRESENTATIVE PORTFOLIO MANAGEMENT MODELS	71
RISK FREE RETURN	79
MARKET RETURN	80
SECURITY RETURNS	85
SUBJECTIVE, NON-LINEAR BETA MODEL	87
FEEDBACK CORRECTION TO SUBJECTIVE FORECASTS	92
OBJECTIVE FUNCTION: VARIANCE	99
REVISION ALGORITHM	111
OBJECTIVE FUNCTION: BETA	115
OBJECTIVE FUNCTION: PRUDENT MAN	119
OBJECTIVE FUNCTION: RETURN	126
OBJECTIVE FUNCTION: QUALITATIVE	126
OBJECTIVE FUNCTION: RANDOM	128
SUMMARY	130

V Evaluation of Alternative Decision Making Systems

INTRODUCTION	131
DATA	132
PERFORMANCE MEASURES	138
STATISTICAL TESTS	142
HYPOTHESIS FORMULATION AND TESTING	145
MANAGEMENT REPORTING SYSTEM	166
SUMMARY	173

VI Conclusion

SUMMARY OF MAJOR FINDINGS	175
FUTURE RESEARCH	178
MANAGEMENT STRATEGY	179

Bibliography	182
Appendix A: Security Universe	187
Appendix B: Symbol Glossary	189
Index	195

*A
New Look at
Portfolio Management*

Chapter I

Introduction

PURPOSE

The purpose of this book is to promote better management of funds by institutional investors. Although the context of this research is academic, its thrust is operational. In this spirit, the tools developed in this study to test hypotheses about alternative approaches to investment management have been designed to fulfill another role as well. They can be used by institutional investors to alter their management styles toward more normative behavior. The primary purpose, therefore, is twofold. On the one hand, it is to evaluate alternative decision-making systems and their consistency with normative investment behavior, and on the other hand, it is to provide a means for institutional investors to improve their management processes.

The research methodology necessary to examine the institutional investment process must include concepts from the behavioral sciences and organization theory as well as financial theory and institutional facts. Even though an analysis of the benefits derived from interdisciplinary approaches to understanding management problems is not the major thrust of this research, this study does offer an excellent opportunity to investigate this approach to solving management problems. A secondary goal therefore, is to demonstrate the power of interdisciplinary methods in analyzing and in building management decision systems.

During the last ten years the primary focus of research in finance has been directed toward developing capital asset pricing theory. The empirical results associated with this effort have strongly supported the economic efficiency of the secondary markets in equity securities. In light of this evidence, the value of the role played by institutional investors in trying to outperform this market has been seriously questioned. While this questioning is valid, particularly so when returns are adjusted for management fees and risk, capital asset pricing theory does not rule out better than market returns for astute investors. In fact it requires these returns to be available to provide an incentive for the market to move toward equilibrium. When one further considers the differences between the downside risk orientation of the fiduciary money manager and the variance of returns, the poor predictive power of Beta models and the strong simplifying assumptions of capital asset pricing theory, the negative implications of capital asset pricing research for institutional investors become very tenuous. A final goal of this research, therefore, is to clarify the distinction between capital asset pricing theory and the realities of pension fund management.

METHODOLOGY

The ultimate focus of this research is on organizational change. Leavitt [46] pictured the major components of organizational change and their interrelationships in the form shown in the following diagram.

Using this framework, it is apparent that tests of alternative organization forms cannot be conducted properly without explicit consideration of the remaining three components. An estimation of the economic value of portfolio management algorithms, for example, without consideration of institutional practices, the incentives for the portfolio manager to use this new tool or his ability to use it would be incomplete. It is in this context that the organizational alternatives examined in this research will be evaluated. The formal research methodologies employed can be broadly defined as Behavioral Science, Management Science and Statistical Hypothesis Testing.

Behavioral Science

Concepts from the Behavioral Sciences will be used primarily to describe and to formalize the practice of pension fund management. Uncertainty absorption, for example, as discussed by Cyert and March [27] can help to explain the prevalence of qualitative vs. quantitative management schemes. Similarly, Simon's [67] discussion of the interrelationship of organizational goals and constraints may be used to substantiate the

Figure 1.1.

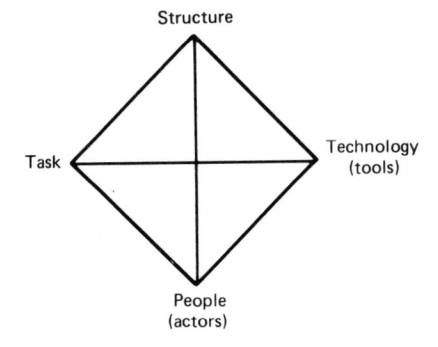

Structure

Task

Technology (tools)

People (actors)

limited use of financial models by institutional investors. One major difficulty, however, is the verification of that process.

In this research, the pension management process is presented in the form of behavioral flow charts. It is not the intent, nor is it within the scope of this research, to convert such flow charts into computer programs for subsequent simulation and analysis [24] [77] [19]. Rather, these charts are intended to provide a reasonable explanation consistent with observed management actions. In fact, the charts presented in Chapter 3 have been viewed by over 500 practicing fund managers and security analysts during the past five years [7] [6] and, at the level of detail considered, have been accepted as faithful representations by this group. In this sense the behavioral processes described in Chapter 3 can be considered as having passed an effective, but informal Turing's test* [76].

Management science

Management Science concepts and tools are examined to determine in what fashion they may be employed to reduce the restrictive influence of certain organizational barriers to effective portfolio management. The triangular distribution is introduced as an important tool to collect subjective forecasts [18] and as a more operational distribution than the normal distribution to provide input to portfolio management algorithms.† The portfolio management problem discussed in Chapter 4 is, as it is in pension fund management, treated as a dynamic multiperiod process. Transaction costs, the quality of input forecasts and feedback corrections are all explicitly included and empirically tested for their respective impact on management decisions.

The data collection phase, which relied heavily on the use of triangular distribution and feedback reports, spanned a period of over three years. This process had important interim educational benefits for the institu-

---

* A behavioral model passes Turing's test when the decisions made by it cannot be distinguished from the decisions generated by the actual behavioral process when both are presented with the same inputs.

†The triangular distribution which can be any triangular shape as opposed to the symmetric, bell shaped, normal distribution, permits the analyst to express forecasts which are skewed optimisticly or pessimisticly. It also incorporates the limited liability of investment securities by not requiring the analyst to assume that he might lose up to an infinite amount.

tion. The relevance for this research, however, is that the forecast distributions used as data in tests of organizational hypotheses have all been used on a daily basis by portfolio managers. From a practical point of view, this is one of the best methods available to insure the reliability of data.

Hypothesis Formulation and testing

One of the most difficult problems encountered was the formulation of important hypotheses about alternative management systems which could also be tested. In my earlier equity valuation research [4], for example, the management implications of the superior performance of earnings and price forecasting models were limited. The equal dollar portfolio selection strategy which did not adjust for risk, however defined, combined with a zero transaction costs assumption substantially narrowed the scope of managerial implications. It was clear from this experience, that an examination of the portfolio management process at the stock selection level would be too narrow. On the other hand, an analysis of the replacement of portfolio managers and security analysts by mechanical rules without consideration of improvements in current practice, would be too general and too extreme to be useful.

In Figure 1.2, the major components of the pension fund management process and the fields of research corresponding to each component are outlined as they exist today. Information below the diagonal in each square represents the primary inputs, and above, the framework in which they are analyzed to produce the necessary information for the next component. From the diagram, it is evident that the Company and Market analysis components supply information, while the Competitive and Planning components evaluate the effectiveness of the process. It is the Decision component, therefore, upon which conclusions about the other steps in the management process will depend. Consequently, it is in this component that hypotheses will be formulated and tested on the relationship between the design of Management Information Systems and the selection of goals for the portfolio management process. The central position of the Decision component makes it very difficult to examine in a real-world context. When the head of the Trust Department at the bank in which the majority of this study was conducted was presented with a proposal which called for test and control groups, the following issues were raised:

1. Analysts covered from 8 to 25 stocks and no stocks were covered by more than one analyst. How could two groups be selected such that

Figure 1.2

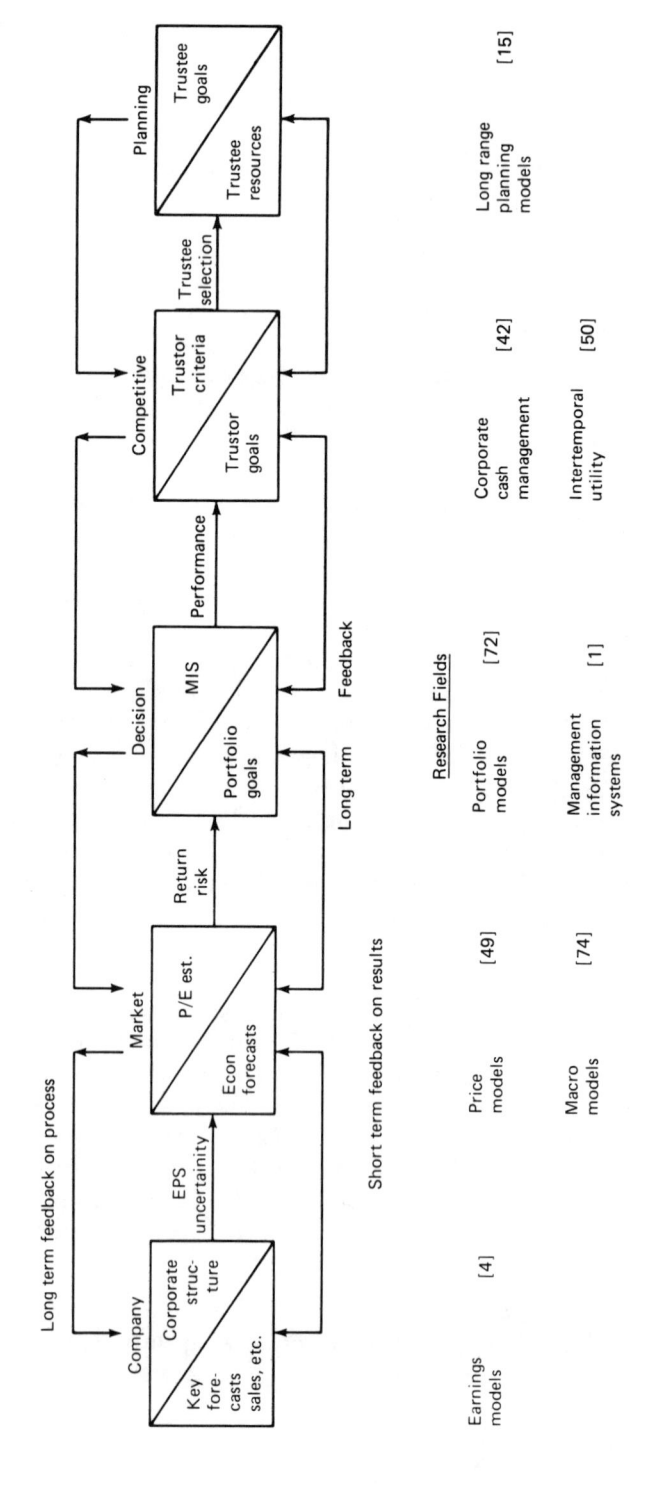

```
Company                Market          Decision  Performance  Competitive  Planning
┌─────────────┐  EPS    ┌─────────────┐ Return   ┌─────────┐ Trustee    ┌─────────┐
│Corporate    │uncer-   │P/E est.     │ risk     │MIS      │ selection  │Trustee  │
│struc-       │tainty   │             │─────────→│         │──────────→ │goals    │
│ture         │────────→│             │          │         │            │         │
│  Key fore-  │         │  Econ       │          │Portfolio│ Trustor    │Trustor  │
│  casts      │         │  forecasts  │          │goals    │ criteria   │resources│
│  sales, etc.│         │             │          │         │            │         │
└─────────────┘         └─────────────┘          └─────────┘ Trustor    └─────────┘
                                                             goals
```

Long term feedback on process

Short term feedback on results   Long term Feedback

Research Fields

| Earnings models [4] | Price models [49] | Portfolio models [72] | Corporate cash management [42] | Long range planning models [15] |
| | Macro models [74] | Management information systems [1] | Intertemporal utility [50] | |

results from one would necessarily have implications for the other and for future investment management?

2. The bank had a responsibility to provide the best management it could for all its customers. If after a year, the very minimum period over which results might be properly evaluated, one group of accounts had significantly different performance from the other, how could these differences be justified to the bank's customers and, under the Prudent Man Principle, perhaps in a court of law?

3. Finally, the traditional skepticism of the experienced manager toward technological innovations surfaced. The management of the Trust Department wondered why, if we were sure our proposals would help improve performance, did we need to test them? And if we were not sure, then we needed to do more research before asking them to participate.

Although the problems encountered in implementing management science concepts will only be discussed peripherally, our experiences were very similar to those summarized by Argyris in his article "Rationality vs Emotionality" [11].

In light of these managerial issues, controlled testing was not attempted. We could have, of course, constructed hypothetical systems to operate in parallel with the actual decision-making system. However, analysts were already under a time constraint. This pressure when added to the knowledge that the test system was not the one on which salaries and promotions would ultimately be based would have made any conclusions reached of questionable reliability.

Our solution was to structure in as much detail as feasible the basic inputs to the revised Decision component. Then, by either aggregating or disaggregating certain elements, the impact of alternative management systems could later be simulated. The principal advantages of this approach are the collection of live data along with the flexibility to evaluate alternative management systems.

Our key assumptions were twofold. One was that analysts, had they actually operated under the proposed alternative systems, would not have systematically altered their inputs. Efforts to assure the validity of this assumption, given evidence that people will bias their forecasts to compensate for inadequacies in their information systems, played a major role in the design of the information collection process. These problems and related issues are discussed in Chapter 3. Secondly and consistent with financial theory, we assumed that when forecasts and goals are properly specified, portfolio management can be reduced to a complex, but tractable mathematical model. The research goals of this paper also require the mathematical model to be general enough to encompass all the alternative goals and management systems under consideration. This is necessary to permit controlled, statistical testing of the joint effects of various management information systems and the form of goal and risk measurements. A general mathematical model is developed in Chapter 4.

In Chapter 5, specific hypotheses about the interaction between management goals and systems are formulated and tested. The general model developed in Chapter 4 is utilized to simulate various goal and system structures. Data are provided by the operational management information system introduced in Chapter 3.

SCOPE

Although there may be broad managerial implications from the results of this research, the scope of this study is limited to an examination of organizational alternatives for fiduciary management and recommendations for subsequent research in financial theory.

Pension funds, due to a combination of rapid growth, large absolute size, management flexibility and legislative concern have been selected as the specific fiduciary management area to be examined. Key problems facing pension fund management are reviewed in Chapter 2. Implications of the results for institutional strategy in the face of a trend toward separate pension fund management firms and guidelines for further research in financial theory are presented in Chapter 6.

A practical reason for limiting the scope is the magnitude of the task involved to test organizational and financial theory using actual decision data without imposing an undue number of simplifying assumptions. If potential selection universes, for example, were limited to only 50 stocks, when many institutions follow over 200, conclusions about the economic added value of pension fund management could be biased negatively [25]. In this study, the selection universe may contain as many as 234 securities. Similarly, if only securities which were in the selection universe for the entire evaluation period were considered, this preselection bias could easily favor pension management performance. In this study securities enter and leave the selection universe in the same manner and with the same timing as they entered and left the approved investment list in the institution which supplied the test data. While this research philosohpy should add to the credence of any results, it also added greatly to the effort necessary to arrive at them. Over eight man-months were required after the research design was established, to verify the thousands of stock price and dividened forecasts, to correct for missing stock splits, etc. and to write and program the many computer systems necessary to carry out the tests.

In summary, the research described in the remaining chapters accepts the constraints imposed when dealing with an ongoing management process in order to generate results which are directly applicable to improving that process. Although this study is directed toward pension fund management processes, it is relevant to all money management firms. The critical issues of how to organize, how to evaluate effectiveness, trading off exposure for return, etc., which are carefully examined in this book, have relevance in all areas of financial management. Finally, due to the major role played by pension funds in the stock market, and the unique source of the forecast data used in this study, conclusions reached should have an important bearing on the direction of future capital asset pricing research.

Chapter 2

Pension Fund Management Environment

Prior to reading about the behavioral analysis of a representative pension fund management process in Chapter 3, it is important to have in mind an overview of recent financial and managerial trends. In addition to supplying such an overview, this chapter also contains a summary of problems external to their own firms confronting pension fund managers.

SIZE AND CONCENTRATION*

Pension trusts were the most rapidly growing segment of fiduciary assets from 1963 to 1971. During this time, pension funds managed by banks increased from approximately 43 to 110.6 billion dollars, an annual compound growth rate of 12.5 percent. The management of these funds is highly concentrated. In 1970, over 75 percent of pension fund assets were managed by only 22 banks. The concentration is even more acute

---

* Institutional figures reported are for the 1970–1971 period over which the tests in this study were conducted. From 1971 through 1974, pension funds managed by banks declined to 73.4 billion, dropping at an annual 9 percent rate. During this same period, funds managed by insurance companies and governmental agencies were growing at about 9 percent. Consistent with the findings of this study, banks during this subsequent period shifted funds from common stocks into less uncertain fixed income securities. Concentration and trading patterns, however, appear to be essentially the same as during the study period. Much of the information in this chapter can be found in the excellent article by Ehrlich [28] on Trust Management.

when one considers that the top two banks manage about 25 percent of the total. In terms of this study, the three firms which permitted the author to review their pension management processes in depth represented 20 percent of the toal market in 1970.

Sheer size alone is only a partial measure of potential market impact or economic relevance. Trading and turnover are equally important factors in the impact equation. In 1971, institutions accounted for over 62 percent of all shares traded on the NYSE and turned their portfolios over 50 percent more frequently than the average for non-institutional investors. Banks represented 38.5 percent of institutional trading. With the next largest group, mutual funds, at only 21.7 percent. Furthermore, within bank trust departments the most active accounts have consistently been pension funds. It is clear from these figures that the high activity levels in pension funds intensifies the real and potential economic impact of their size and concentration characteristics.

Another facet of size and concentration involves the distribution of trustees. Approximately 90 percent of all pension funds over 50 million dollars are managed by banks. The result of this twofold concentration is that the future value of pension benefits small number of portfolio managers who in turn are selected by a similarly limited number of corporate or union officials.

This fact, as well as the implications for corporate control, have not gone unrecognized. In the February 1972 *Financial Executive*, the following statement appeared quoting Soldofsky [35],

> The banks exert more power or influence over business than the other financial intermediaries. The range and resources of banking power are augmented strongly by their growing business in pension funds. Such growing and concentrated financial power is inconsistent with our very deeply rooted value system. Banks aggrevate this problem by their secretiveness about the extent of their stock holdings.

Pension funds managed by banks, the focus of this research, are therefore the major single investor group in the stock market and because of their size, concentration, activity and potential power, a major issue in themselves.

INVESTMENT POLICY

Whatever return goals may be set for a pension fund, the decisions made by portfolio managers are tightly constrained by the "Prudent Man

Principle." Farnum, [31] who at the time was in charge of the largest pension fund management department in the United States, stated the Prudent Man Principle as:

> The time tested standard is that a trustee is required to employ such diligence and such prudence in the care and management of trust property as in general prudent men of discretion and intelligence employ in their own affairs. A bank trustee may in some important respects be held to an even higher degree of care since it holds itself out to be an expert and because it is better equipped than the ordinary man.

In his section on Investments, he made additional comments on prudent investments and outlined some of the risks in not investing prudently.

> Pension and profit sharing trusts make no distinction between principle and income. Typically, the modern trust agreement gives the bank broad powers of investment. Irrespective of these broad powers, the common law of prudence governs the actions of the trustee.
>
> State laws protect the trust beneficiary. For instance, in New York State, section 100-b of the banking law provides that all investments by a bank shall be at its sole risk, and the capital stock, property and effects of the bank shall be liable for losses, unless the investments are proper and permitted in the trust instrument.

The notion that the bank is directly liable for all breaches in prudent policy has been institutionalized for all members of the Federal Reserve system. Member banks are expected to have capital, in addition to all other capital requirements, sufficient to cover claims under the Prudent Man Principle up to 200 percent of gross trust department earnings. This would normally amount to 5 percent to 15 percent of the entire capital account.

The American Institute of Banking emphasized in 1954 the importance of the safety aspect of the Prudent Man Principle in the following excerpt from its publication, *Trust Department:*

> *Services: Trusts I* [10]
> The trust institution, however, not only would fail to perform its duty but would soon lose its trust business if it failed to employ the trust property in such a way as to produce the best return obtainable with safety...

A recent article by Belliveau [18] in the *Institutional Investor* indicates that safety may have become the prime consideration of portfolio managers. The subtitle, "It's just possible a manager can be sued even if the endowment is up," refers to the growing number of law suits which seek to hold portfolio managers responsible for losses on individual stocks regardless of overall portfolio performance. The extent of the difference between normative portfolio theory and the practice of pension fund management within current legal boundaries can be seen in the following statement by Belliveau: "While most trust lawyers still maintain that trustees will be held liable for each security, a few exceptions have cropped up in the courts over the years." She goes on to discuss the possibility that these exceptions along with recent articles in law journals favoring portfolio theory may lay the groundwork for eventual redefinition of Prudent Man requirements to be consistent with modern portfolio theory. It is apparent, therefore, that at least one of the reasons pension fund managers have made little use of mean-variance portfolio tools is that they may lead to investment decisions which could result in successful malfeasance suits against the managers and their organizations.

PEOPLE IN PENSION FUND MANAGEMENT

The thrust in this research is directed toward changing the portfolio management process. It is the people who direct and carry out this process whose behavior is under analysis and who will bear the effects of any changes to be made. Their receptivity to change, combined with the competitive pressures external to the bank and the organization pressures within the bank will determine whether or not any change occurs at all.

Growth in this industry has not been restricted to the number of dollars managed. Rough estimates show the number of security analysts and portfolio managers increased by a factor of four during the 1960s. In a survey conducted by a personnel firm during May and June 1969 [53], the following characteristics were observed for the 493 analysts and managers who responded:

BANKS
    23.5% were employed by banks
        Banks along with Insurance and Educational institutions were the lowest paying, falling at about 50% of the salaries in investment banking and brokerage.

EDUCATION
    93.5% had at least one degree
    46.0% had a master's degree
    5.2% had a doctorate

The incidence of an advanced degree varied less than 10% between the ages of 25 and 50.

Over 50% of the analysts working in banks stated that their firms did not provide in-house training and that they would like such training.

AGE

Length of service with the same employer is bi-modal with peaks at 2-4 years and 10-15 years. The median age is between 30 and 34 years. The average age is 40.7 years.

How does the analyst view his profession? From time to time there are revealing personal interviews published in the *Wall Street Journal*. On January 23, 1968, the following statements were printed about a Mr. Samson Coslow who had switched from song writing to security analysis in 1961.

> In switching, careers, Mr. Coslow got into one of the financial community's fastest-growing professions—and one that has defied attempts to reduce it to a science that can be taught. Success comes as often to the newcomer with judgment and intuition as to the man who has immersed himself in the field for years.

This imposing tone had changed drastically after the sharp market turn-around in the early 70's and the failure and fire sale acquisitions of a number of brokerage firms. In another *Wall Street Journal* article on August 31, 1972, Roger Murray judged the state of the art, categorized by judgment and intuition in 1968, as "lousy." He went on to encourage specialization and hard detailed work. "Those that are going to make it will do so by developing a distinctive expertise, by becoming recognized as particularly outstanding in certain areas." The analyst whose career was the subject of the column, stated as his most important reason for being a security analyst, the following: "If analysts are influential in establishing values of companies that are proper values, then the allocation of our nation's resources should be more productive, right?"

The security analyst, if the quotes above are representative, has gone on the defensive. A lot of the glamour in his profession has disappeared along with many brokerage firms and the notion of an ever rising DOW. The relevance of this change in attitude is that it may not only make the analyst ready to accept change, particularly if it is viewed as rational and analytical, but according to Cyert and March [27], current problems in his profession will cause the analyst to begin searching for change. One of the first steps in changing any management process is, of course, for the participants to learn about new ideas. According to the survey made in 1969, bank security analysts even then appeared receptive to learning about new techniques. In addition, the very high educational level for this profession would seem to indicate a ready capacity to assimilate new concepts.

On the other hand, there is another side to this issue. The bi-modal age distribution tends to be accentuated in banks due in part to their lower than average salary levels at the time of this survey. This gives rise to a situation in which new analysts with few vested interests and fresh from receiving their MBA's, argue for more sophisticated systems than those proposed by the management scientist. Older analysts counter that new proposals are too radical and ignore the good features of current practices which they have spent their careers developing. Without the influence of middle aged managers to provide compromise, such conflict could easily forestall any changes. The high educational level also ensures that when criticisms are lodged against change proposals, they will be articulate and not "straw men" to be easily discarded.

EXTERNAL PRESSURES FOR CHANGE

External pressures from corporate treasurers, academic researchers and even the U.S. Government for fundamental changes in the portfolio management process have mounted during the last five years. Indeed the vast majority of the literature in the field, from the performance evaluation of Sharpe [62] and Treynor [75] to the headline in the *Wall Street Journal* on June 7, 1974, which read:

Bye - Bye, Go - Go?
More Money Managers Now Aim Just to Match
Popular Market Indexes
They See Efforts to Select "Winners" as Futile

questions the economic validity of the portfolio management process. It is beyond the scope of this work to review this critique along all its dimensions. Certain dimensions, however, such as the alternative proposed by the *Wall Street Journal* headline, which are examined and tested in subsequent chapters of this study are outlined below.

Market Efficiency

The market efficiency argument states that the stock market is sufficiently competitive and hence the presence of special knowledge which could lead to abnormally high profits sufficiently rare to make it very unlikely for any money manager to consistently outperform the market as a whole. Studies of the mutual fund industry by Jensen [44], Sharpe [62], Treynor [75] and many others all support the notion of market efficiency and its performance implications.

Sharpe [62] reinforced the implications for performance by showing that one of the best predictors of future mutual fund performance is based on the ratio of management expenses to assets. This is, of course, exactly what one would expect if investment performance were limited by market efficiency to meeting the averages.

By 1973 at least two pension fund management firms, Wells Fargo Bank and Battery March, had accepted this view and were offering index matching funds. They also significantly lowered their management fees for these funds, since high cost analysts and portfolio managers will not be required. Although neither of these firms was a major force in the industry, the challenge to the industry leaders was clear. In the words of the April 29, 1973, *New York Times* article which reviews this issue, "In effect, Battery March and Wells Fargo have thrown down the gauntlet." This article also suggests that many portfolio managers have come to accept this position themselves. When a hand vote was taken to determine return goals at a January 1973 conference attended by 700 pension fund administrators, the dominant figure was 9 percent. As the article points out this is very close to the 9.3 percent average market return from 1926 to 1965 found by Lorie and Fisher in a University of Chicago study.

By 1975, after a halting start, the trend toward matching the indicies gained momentum. A November 12, 1975, *Wall Street Journal* article entitled "On the Average," reported shifts of trial amounts by such giant funds as AT & T, Ford Motor and EXXON into index funds. Justifying the goal of being only average, one corporate executive was quoted as saying "We made the move to index funds because we concluded that it was silly to spend a lot of money on management fees, performance studies and trading commissions when our money managers haven't beaten the market anyway."

Performance Measurement

The development of performance measurement theory and tools was a logical consequence to the notion of market efficiency. This development has progressed along three principal dimensions: competitive analyses, academic research, and work by the banking industry toward the establishment of measurement standards.

Although a number of firms analyze the performance of pension fund managers, A. G. Becker and Co. [2], with over 1,500 pension funds covering over $40 billion in assets, is by far the largest and most comprehensive firm in this field. A. G. Becker's position virtually forces bank pension fund managers to provide all the data necessary to compute performance measurements requested by corporate treasurers. Failure to comply would, of course, be interpreted negatively by corporate treasurers and could easily precipitate a transfer of funds out of the bank to a competitor who had agreed to be evaluated. The assumption behind this demand by corporate treasurers is that relative preformance measured by A. G. Becker over past decisions is indicative of likely future relative performance. How valid is this assumption? In an unpublished study by A. G. Becker of its proprietary data, over 200 funds were divided into four quartiles ranging from the highest to the lowest returns from 1966 to 1969. If past relative performance measures were indicative of future relative performance, then one would expect significantly more than 25 percent of the funds in each quartile to remain in that quartile during subsequent periods. In fact, when these rankings were compared to those computed for 1969–1971, the number of funds remaining in each quartile was *not* significantly different from 25 percent. Based on A. G. Becker's data for the periods covered, the corporate treasurer's needed assumption of stability appears to be invalid.

In an era of high interest rates and rapidly rising operating costs, the failure of a pension fund to generate returns anticipated by a corporate treasurer can have a substantial negative impact on corporate cash flows and profits. The bank pension fund manager, therefore, finds himself under great pressure to live up to or to improve his performance. Unfortunately, he also finds his usually long term investment policies measured on a quarterly basis in terms specified by A. G. Becker, which appear to be largely irrelevant to his probable future performance. These external pressures are further augmented when he considers the implications of a 1970 survey by Louis Harris Associates which found that the percentage of large nonfinancial corporations selecting banks to manage their pension funds had declined from 67 percent in 1960 to 39 percent in 1970.

Academic researchers would criticize the A. G. Becker results for their failure to incorporate a specific correction for risk. Substantial academic effort has been devoted to the development of risk adjusted performance measures based on the capital asset pricing models introduced by Sharpe [61] and Lintner [48] in the mid-1960s. It is beyond the scope of this book to summarize or to critically examine this large body of literature. The reader is referred to Sharpe [63], Blume [38] and Fama [30]. However, certain aspects of this research are relevant in a discussion of external pressures on portfolio managers. During the last half of the 1960s, β adjusted performance measures were incorporated into A. G. Becker's evaluations and used on a broad basis throughout the pension fund industry [3]. The essence of β risk adjustment stems from Sharpe's market model:

$$R_s = \alpha_s + \beta_s R_m + e \qquad (1)$$

where R_s = security return
R_m = equity market return
α_s = market independent return
β_s = market dependent return factor
e = equation error

In (1) there are theoretically two sources of risk-variations in R_m and in the magnitude of e. In reality, there are many other sources, e.g. inability to estimate α or β well, the presence of economic factors beyond R_m, etc. By diversifying with as few as a dozen randomly selected securities, the effect of e can be drastically reduced. The β_p for the portfolio, however, is a weighted average of the β_s's in the portfolio and is not reduced by diversification. β_s is usually defined, therefore, as the "systematic" or "nondiversifiable" risk. Theoretically, in an efficient market there should be no return for diversifiable risk and there should be sufficient return to compensate for nondiversifiable risk. This is the essence behind the Sharpe-Lintner market equilibrium equation;

$$\bar{R}_p - R_f = \beta_p (\bar{R}_m - R_f) \qquad (2)$$

where $\bar{R}_p$ = expected portfolio return
R_f = risk free rate
$\bar{R}_m$ = expected market return

If we divide both sides of (2) by β_p, we obtain on the left Treynor's widely used risk adjusted return measure:

$$\frac{R_p - R_f}{\beta_p} = R_m - R_f \qquad (3)$$

where R_p and R_m are ex post realized returns.

Superior management would turn (3) into an inequality with the left hand side greater than the right. Inferior performance would result in just the opposite. Unfortunately for pension fund managers, when management fees and expenses are taken into account, virtually all studies indicate inferior performance [62] [75] [44]. These results are not dependent upon Treynor's measure, but hold as well for Sharpe's measure,

$$\frac{R_p - R_f}{\sigma_p} \tag{4}$$

where σ_p is the standard deviation of portfolio returns and Jensen's measure:

$$R_p - R_f - \beta_p(R_m - R_f) \tag{5}$$

Do these measures exhibit better predictive behavior than pure return analysis? According to Sharpe [62] who examined mutual fund performance between 1944 and 1963 the answer is "yes." Unfortunately Sharpe's tests are only for mutual funds, do not even include pension funds, and are over a different time period than the A. G. Becker tests.

On a more fundamental level, do these one-parameter risk measures accurately adjust for risk? Friend and Blume in 1970 [38] reached the following conclusion based on studies of 200 random portfolios composed of selections from 788 stocks traded on the New York Stock Exchange between 1960 and 1968. "The Sharpe, Treynor and Jensen one parameter measures of portfolio performance based on this theory seem to yield seriously biased estimates of performance, with the magnitudes of the bias related to portfolio risk." A recent follow-up study by Klemkosky [45] using mutual fund performance over the period 1966–1971, reached a similar conclusion, "The composite performance measures, especially the Treynor and Jensen measures, were biased in a positive direction." The irony of this finding is that riskier funds would tend to have their performance over-stated and more conservative funds such as pension portfolios would be put at a relative disadvantage.

Finally, it is important in the context of pressures on the pension fund manager to note that although β_p's have been shown to be reasonably stable for a given portfolio from year to year [47], β_s's are usually very unstable over similar periods. Mlynarczyk in 1972 [55] stated in reference to β_s and α_s, "Betas and alphas are not stable over time. The point is that betas and alphas measured from the past provide little, if any, information about the future—regardless of the time span used to develop the estimates."

As a further illustration of β_s instability, thirty β_s's and their standard errors of estimation were randomly selected from the Butcher and Sherrerd estimates of β_s and α_s for 2,321 stocks over fifty-two weeks during

1970 and 1971. The average ratio of the standard error in estimating β_s to the value of β_s is .42. The theory underlying β risk adjustment assumes that this ratio is 0. Based on these statistics, if the portfolio manager were considering a security with an estimated β_s of 1 (in order to move his portfolio closer to the market), he could be no more than 95 percent confident that the true value would be included in a range of .18 to 1.82. Unfortunately, this range is so broad that it includes everything from very defensive to very aggressive securities. This large uncertainty compounds the task of the portfolio manager whose job it is to make marginal changes in his portfolios based on estimates of β_s. Long term, stable β_p's on fixed portfolios, therefore, are of little value to the portfolio manager who is frequently evaluated on a quarterly basis and whose decision parameters are in terms of β_s not β_p.

The Bank Administration Institute's report [12] [13] on recommendations for the measurement of pension fund performance is the third major dimension of performance measurement pressures on pension fund managers. This report is composed of two major sections. The first provides a method for computing return, not considering risk, which is independent of the timing of contributions to the fund and withdrawals from it. The philosophy of the approach is important. Its goal is to identify the return achieved through the pension fund managers' actions, independent of lucky or unlucky timing of corporate interaction with the fund. Theoretically, if a fund could be valued at every contribution or withdrawal and a time weighted geometric return computed over all such periods, no problems would exist. In practice, however, the frequency of corporate interaction and number of funds managed could easily incur an operational cost which would exceed any return gains. The first part of the BAI report, therefore, devotes itself to finding efficient means to estimate market values and resulting time weighted returns.

The pressures on pension fund managers arising out of this portion of the BAI report are due largely to the shock effect present when any new and quantified grading system is introduced into an established, qualitative process.

The second portion of the BAI report deals with adjusting time weighted returns for risk exposure. This section is theoretical and is more concerned with making a case for risk adjustment than examining operational procedures to accomplish it. Its foundations are in the cited studies by Sharpe, Treynor, Jensen and Fama. The final statement of this section in fact appeals to the essence of the Sharpe-Lintner equation (2). "The main point of this supplement is simply that if the market on average pays premiums for risk bearing, then risk must somehow be important information in explaining portfolio performance." What additional pressures does this second section of the BAI report place upon pension fund managers? In fairness to the report, its risk adjustment recommendations were made prior to the published results of Blume and Klemkosky. Nevertheless, it is still probably true that corporate treasurers are much more aware of the BAI recommendations than they are aware of any failures of risk measures suggested by BAI to hold up in practice.

Several quotes from the BAI report are helpful in establishing whether or not the proposed measures are even theoretically, if not operationally, relevant to pension fund performance.

> Is the theory of pension fund portfolio performance presented in the last section suitable for practical application? We should note at the outset that to date this theory has only been applied to evaluate the performance of mutual funds, most notably by Jensen.
>
> Finally, the available literature on formal portfolio theories is exclusively concerned with optimal portfolio decisions by risk-adverse individual investors; there is no systematic treatment of the problem of optimal portfolio decisions by institutions.
>
> In particular, there is currently no theoretical reason for concluding that a pension fund should hold an efficient and thus highly diversified portfolio.

The first and second quotes are inconsistent. The first refers to a "theory of pension fund portfolio performance" while the latter states that no such theory exists. The third quote questions the theoretical relevance of the Sharpe-Lintner equation to the composition of pension portfolios. Yet all the performance measures suggested by the report are derived from this equation. Finally, the first quote points out that the theory has only been tested on mutual funds.

Pension fund managers, therefore, are under pressure to justify performance in terms of risk adjusted measures which in themselves have not been justified for pension fund management either theoretically or empirically. Furthermore, given the relative complexity for most pension fund managers of the mathematical foundations underlying these measures, it is difficult, if not impossible, for them to question their appropriateness.

Summary

From the data presented in this chapter, it is apparent that pension fund management is a major financial industry experiencing external pressures for change. While these external pressures may be strong, it is not clear that they are justified in terms of current evidence or theory. In spite of this, or more probably due to an inability to critique, pension fund managers have in general acknowledged many negative judgments and in certain cases, such as Wells Fargo Bank, have changed their management goals accordingly.

In the context of Leavitt's components of organizational change in Figure 1.1, this chapter has reviewed the Tasks facing pension fund managers and the people who comprise this profession. In the next chapter, the third component—Organization—and the fourth component—Technology—are examined.

Chapter 3

Organizational Analysis

This chapter presents both formal and functional descriptions of representative pension fund management processes. These desciptions provide the starting point for the development and testing of new management systems which may be better able to cope with the external pressures discussed in Chapter 2. An example of a new functional system which has been installed and used by a major institution is described as well. The design of this system indicates the initial steps an institution might take in attempting to alter its management systems.

All pressures on pension fund managers are not externally generated. In this chapter, internal pressures perceived by managers as well as responsibilities and hence internal pressures avoided by them are examined in relation to their impact on the quality of decision-making. Although the functional models presented in this chapter have not been turned into computer programs and tested to see if they could be statistically rejected,* they have all been developed in close cooperation with

---

*The usual practice in classical statistics is to specify a null or no difference hypothesis and then test to determine if this statement can be rejected. Unless all possible alternatives for the true but unknown parameters are stated, however, it is not possible to draw probabilistic conclusions about accepting the hypothesis. Although "null hypothesis testing," as this procedure is called, may be appropriate for many problems, its value in establishing the truthfulness of organization structures is limited at best. Turing's test which is not a classical statistics procedure, but which is directed toward conformance vs rejection, would appear more appropriate. Other organization researchers, for example Clarkson in his behavioral analysis of personal trust management [24] or Van Horn in his article titled "Validation of Simulation Results" [77], have reached similar conclusions.

security analysts and portfolio managers in pension fund management and critically reviewed by them. The theoretical validity is enhanced by the observation that many of the behavioral phenomena, which from a theoretical point of view should be present, are easily identifiable in the behavioral flow charts. In addition, there is a close agreement between behavioral flow charts of pension fund management drawn by different researchers working in different institutions at different points in time.

FORMAL ORGANIZATION

When most managers hear the word "organization" the concept of an organization chart quickly comes into mind. In the various institutions in which this research was conducted, the senior executive in the pension fund management area was asked to provide a description of his organization. Invariably the first document offered was a formal organization chart. Such charts have a twofold relevance to this research. One, they demonstrate the close similarity among major institutions in this regard and thereby reinforce the implication that institutions are more alike than they are different in their approaches to pension fund management. Secondly, they represent one of the major constraints to change, since substantive changes to formal organization structures tend to be difficult and lengthy processes.

The organization charts in Figures 3.1, 3.2 and 3.3 below have been redrawn from the originals to delete names of officers and to achieve a consistent level of detail. With the exception of these modifications they correspond directly to the organization charts of the respective institutions during the period 1968–1971. In order to preserve the anonymity of the institutions involved (a necessary requirement imposed by each institution) the charts are identified by letter only. The institutions represented are:

Bank of New York, New York
Bankers Trust Company, New York
Chase Manhattan Bank, New York
Mellon National Bank and Trust Company, Pittsburgh
Morgan Guarantee Trust Company, New York
First National Bank and Trust Company, Chicago

Many of the banks are so similar at the level of detail considered, to allow representation by the same organization chart. Comparison of the three organization variations also reveals the following common structures:

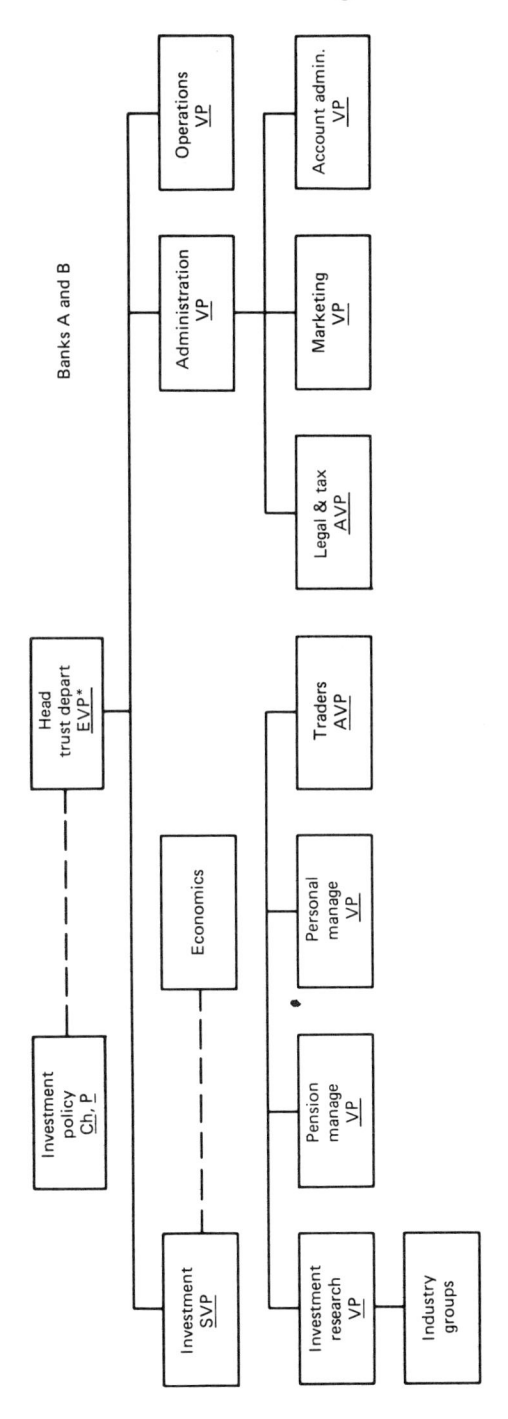

Organizational Analysis / 27

Figure 3.1

28 / *A New Look at Portfolio Management*

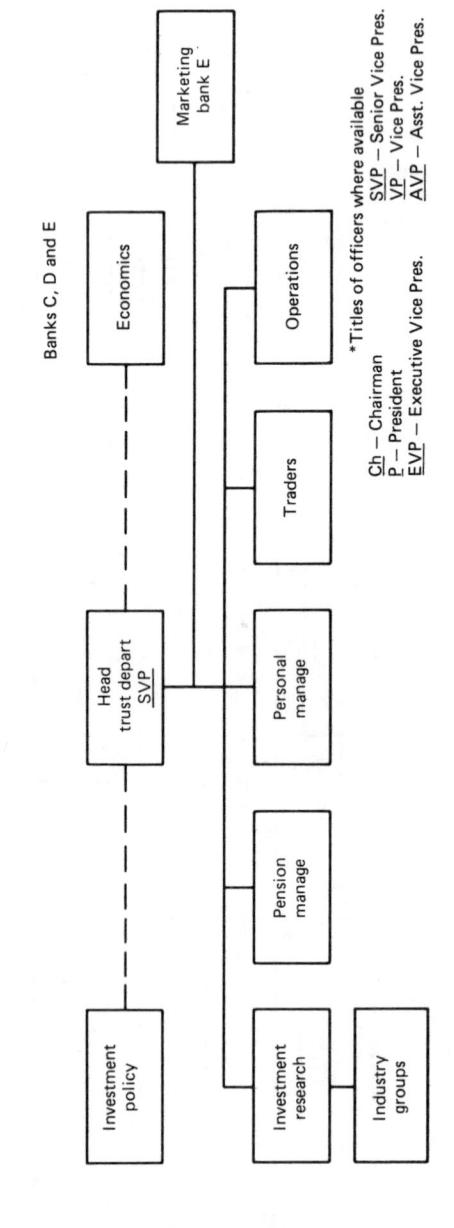

Figure 3.2

Banks C, D and E

*Titles of officers where available
Ch – Chairman
P – President
EVP – Executive Vice Pres.
SVP – Senior Vice Pres.
VP – Vice Pres.
AVP – Asst. Vice Pres.

- Marketing bank E
- Economics
- Operations
- Traders
- Head trust depart SVP
- Personal manage
- Pension manage
- Investment policy
- Investment research
- Industry groups

Organizational Analysis / **29**

Figure 3.3

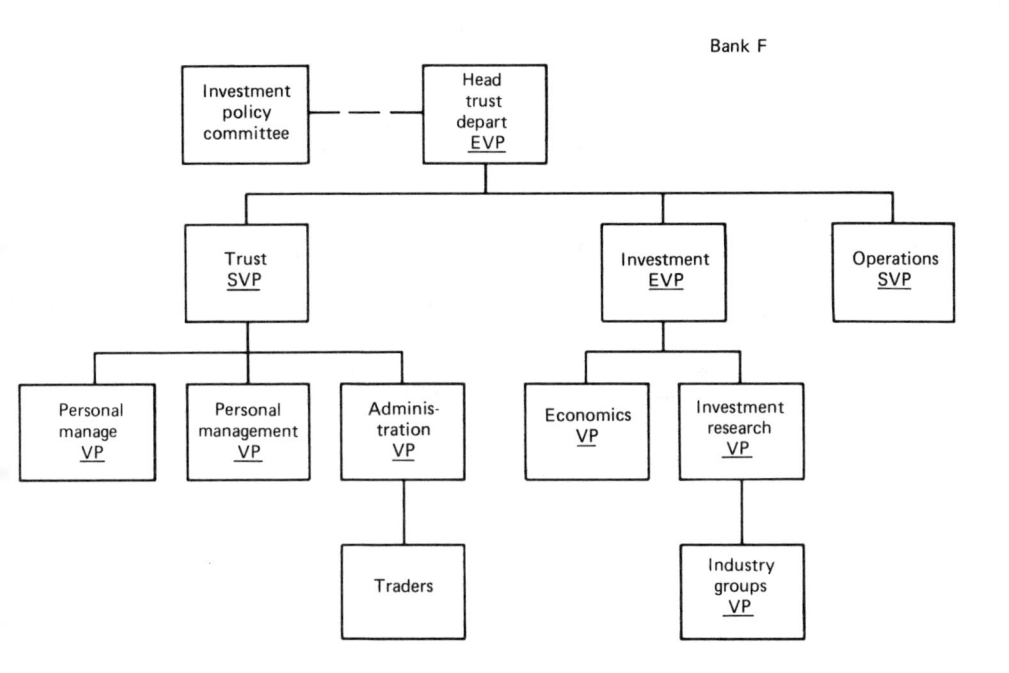

Bank F

- Investment policy committee
- Head trust depart EVP
  - Trust SVP
    - Personal manage VP
    - Personal management VP
    - Administration VP
      - Traders
  - Investment EVP
    - Economics VP
    - Investment research VP
      - Industry groups VP
  - Operations SVP

1. Pension and Personal portfolio management are always different departments.
2. Investment research or security analysis is always separate from portfolio management and organized by industry groups.
3. Traders are always separate from security analysts and portfolio managers.
4. The Administrative staffs whose primary role is to maintain day-to-day contact with trust customers are always separate from the security analysts, traders and portfolio managers.

Differences are confined primarily to the location of Administration, e.g. customer contact and staff support functions, the level at which economic support is provided and the span of control by the Trust Department Head.

Although the relevance of the formal organizations to the decision-making processs will be clearer later, several points can be made now. For example, the individual entrepreneur of capital asset pricing theory underlying performance measurement has no counterpart in the institutions considered. It might be argued that the Head of the Trust Department fulfills this function. However, his role is managerial not operational, and in only a very remote way could he help the stock market reach equilibrium. The assumption made in the BAI study that theory developed for the personal investor could be used in pension fund investment contrasts with the separation of these functions in every institution examined.* Finally, the formal organization structure employed by each institution does not appear to be related to size or location. One of the smallest banks, for example, had the same structure as one of the largest, and a New York bank had the same organization as a Chicago bank.

FUNCTIONAL ORGANIZATION

The purpose of a functional organization chart is to describe how an organization actually works. Figure 3.4 is a general representation of a functional organization chart which is consistent with more explicit variations in the literature of organization theory [1] [27].

---

*There are a number of reasons for this separation. Personal trusts, for example, are taxed while pension trusts are not. The predominant customer in personal trust is the widow, while in pension trust it is the corporate treasurer calling for different marketing strategies and staffing.

Figure 3.5 is a behavioral flow chart of one of the two major forms of pension fund management used by institutions in this study. Diamonds are intended to point out areas which are more decision-making than processing oriented. Rectangles illustrate the latter. Dashed lines indicate feedback flows. The general framework in Figure 3.4 has been superimposed, showing each of the basic components to be represented. The process depicted, however, is tactical and excludes any strategic planning activities. In terms of the five components of pension fund management in Figure 1.2, therefore, only the first four are included. Figure 3.5 is also a historic document in terms of this research. It is a copy of a slide made in 1968 for an executive meeting with the head of a major trust department. The issues raised by an analysis of this slide subsequently lead to fundamental changes in the functional organization of this department and, as a byproduct, generated the data for this research. This slide is historic in another context as well. It has been critically viewed by many corporate treasurers, security analysts, portfolio managers and investment executives since 1968 [6], [7], [8], [9]. Transcripts of questions by audiences following these presentations are limited to efforts to extend the chart to cover their own institutions and do not appear to take issue with the structure shown. Although some steps in Figure 3.5 were unique at the time to one institution, most were found in all the institutions examined. The common functional steps in the pension fund management processes are outlined below.

P/E and Earnings per Share Forecasting

Future prices were forecasted by combining separately estimated price earnings ratios and earnings figures.*

$$\hat{P}_t = (P/E)_t \, \hat{E}_t, \tag{6}$$

where t = forecast horizon, usually between 6 and 18 months,

$\hat{P}_t$ = estimated price in t periods

$(P/E)_t$ = estimated P/E in t periods **

$\hat{E}_t$ = estimated earnings per share in t periods

*The past tense is used through the behavioral description since the author does not wish to imply that current management systems are exactly the same as those studied between 1968 and 1971.

**This estimate was frequently made conditional upon the forecasted P/E_x for one of the market indexes, for example the DOW. In this event, (6) becomes:

$$\hat{P}_t = (P/E|P/E_x)_t \, \hat{E}_t \tag{7}$$

Figure 3.4

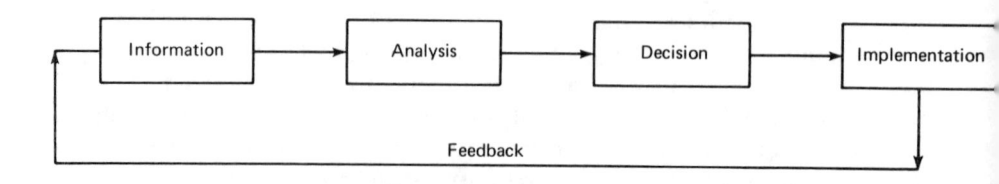

Information → Analysis → Decision → Implementation

Feedback

Organizational Analysis / **33**

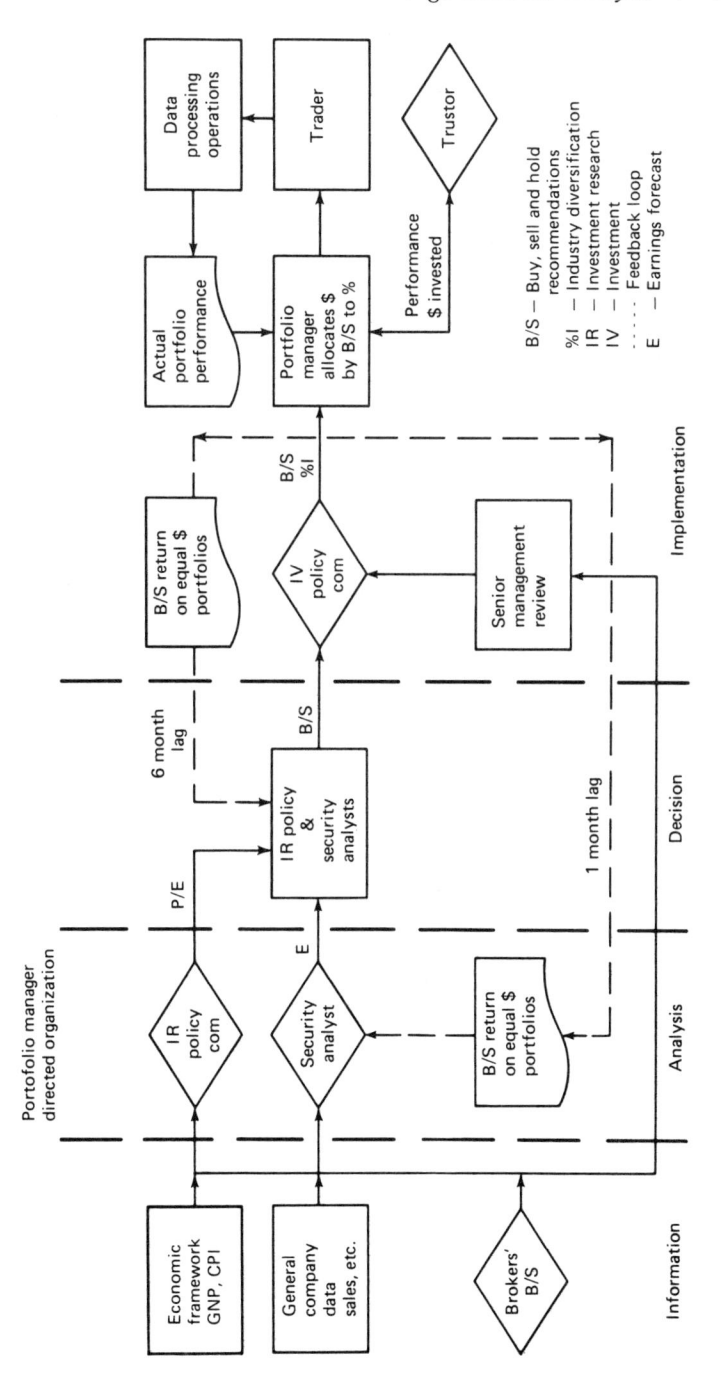

Figure 3.5

34 / A New Look at Portfolio Management

Analysts refer to this as a market relative.

Many institutions made this forecasting method official policy. For example, one institution stated the following in an internal policy document:

> First, our general theory is based on the belief that stock prices and movements are functions of earnings and rationally applied multiples, rather than technical patterns, emotional factors and the like. Second, there is a belief that there is a proper P/E (multiple) which reflects a company's quality, stability, growth, scarcity, variation of earnings from the trend, dividends and other factors.

This two-component, one-stock-at-a-time method of forecasting is shown in the analysis portion of Figure 3.5. The IR Policy diamond indicates that a policy committee comprised of the management of the Investment Research Department was responsible for supplying the P/E estimate.

At this point, it is important to bear in mind that regardless of the economic or statistical merits of (6), the unanimity of this approach among pension fund managers makes it a significant factor in the market and in the analysis of pension management systems.

Qualitative Recommendations

Using $\hat{P}_t$ from (6), future returns were estimated by:

$$\hat{R}_t = \left(\frac{\hat{P}_t - P_o}{t\, P_o}\right) n + \hat{d}_t \qquad (8)$$

where t = length of the forecast period
$\hat{R}_t$ = estimated annual return over next t periods
P_o = current price
n = number of periods per year, e.g. if t were in terms of months, n = 12
$\hat{d}_t$ = estimated annual dividend return, usually just the current annual dividend divided by P_o

Then depending on the magnitude of $\hat{R}_t$ and its algebraic sign combined with an assessment of the reliability of $\hat{P}_t$, a qualitative Buy, Sell or Hold decision was made. This was usually done by a committee which met once or twice a week to consider a formal agenda of five to ten stocks with others treated on a much more cursory basis as necessary. Some institutions used Favorable, Unfavorable and Neutral as classifications, while others assigned a + or − to the Neutral or Hold classification. Regardless of the terms employed, however, all institutions translated return estimates into qualitative rankings. Ordinal scales established in this way ranged from three points for the basic Buy-Hold-Sell to no more than nine points for the most complex systems.

Industry Diversification

All institutions in this study sought to achieve diversification by setting policies which would limit the maximum percentage of a fund which could be invested in the same industry. Similar diversification is legally required for Common Trust Funds, e.g. funds in which multiple pension funds might hold shares or units, by the Controller of the Currency. In Regulation 9 of the Trust Powers of National Banks [26] holdings of any given stock are limited to the lesser of "20% of the value of the Common Trust Fund" or "5% of the number of such shares outstanding." Diversification limits were set by the Investment Policy Committee represented by IV POLICY in Figure 3.5 and shown in Figures 3.1, 3.2 and 3.3

Management Review

Regulation 9 holds the board of directors "—responsible for the investment of trust funds by the bank" and requires that, "All investments of trust funds by the trust department of every such national bank shall be made, retained or disposed of only with the approval of the trust investment committee." Thus the Investment Policy Committee shown in Figure 3.5, not only sets diversification limits, but fulfills a regulatory requirement in addition by reviewing all qualitative recommendations and either accepting or changing them. Given the responsibility charged to the board of directors along with the allocation of capital required by the Federal Reserve to cover potential losses, it is not surprising to find a senior management review of investment policy committee actions.

Portfolio Allocation

Pension fund managers in large institutions may be responsible for fifty or more accounts. Many managers argue that to be fair to all accounts, good buys should be prorated over each of them. Consequently, after buys and sells have been selected, managers frequently find, given industry constraints, that the actual portfolio management task has become an arithmetic allocation problem. Indeed, many institutions employ clerical support personnel to do this job. The portfolio manager, therefore, is represented by a rectangle in Figure 3.5 in keeping with the convention of using this form to indicate essentially processing operations.

Performance Reports

There was a wide range of performance reports in the institutions covered. However, all had at least some form of equal dollar analysis. In this type of feedback report, the percent returns (ignoring transaction costs, management fees and operating expenses) are averaged for each qualitative grouping. The return computed is equivalent to having invested an equal dollar amount in each security in each group. The numbers on the dashed lines give the number of months between when a recommendation was made and when an analysis of the actual performance was received. The portfolio performance reports received by the portfolio manager and the trustor had a number of different statistics such as capital appreciation, income yield, etc., but all included the BAI time weighted return or an approximation, for example, the Financial Executives Measure. In addition to these measures, performance reports prepared by A. G. Becker contained variants of the Sharpe, Treynor and Jensen risk-adjusted performance measures. There is, of course, much more to the functional pension fund management process than this brief overview contains. Not presented, for example, is the structure of meetings in which security analysts attempted to sell their ideas to critical portfolio managers and policy committees. Allocation of commission dollars to obtain recommendations from brokers is shown in Figure 3.5, but not treated in detail. Figure 3.5 does, nevertheless, provide sufficient functional structure to address the central management problems and alternatives.

Management Analysis of Management Problems

Before examining from a behavioral science viewpoint the internal pressures generated by this form of the functional organization, it is instructive to review several self-analyses by pension fund managers. Cantor in a 1968 article entitled, "Why Banks Have Trouble Managing Investment Accounts" [21], highlighted three reasons, "too much money," "archaic decision making," and "shuffling accounts." Fiske in another *Institutional Investor* article in 1969, [36] gave as his reasons for the decline of the two top funds in overall return in 1968 to 301 and 303 out of

310 in 1969 as, " . . . Size. The two problems are the size of the money managed and the size of the staff assembled to do it." Judged by these remarks and critical quotes mentioned earlier, the effectiveness of the process generalized in Figure 3.5 was clearly in question both internally and externally. The next section examines the ability of management to respond to these issues through the organization forms just described.

BEHAVIORAL ANALYSIS

The framework proposed by Leavitt in Figure 1.1 shows organization structure as a key component of organizational change, but it does not elaborate on the *way* organization structure facilitates organizational change. Cyert and March [27] have tackled this problem and used a basic feedback-control system approach to deal with it. Many other organization theorists have also addressed this area [64].

The Cyert and March framework is both consistent with these other theories and lends itself to the management decision system orientation of this study. Cyert and March have summarized the primary components and interrelationships of their descriptive theory of organization change in the form of a flow chart. This flow chart is reproduced in Figure 3.6.

In the context of this study Figure 3.6 serves as a reference point. The functional flow in Figure 3.5 will be compared to the information and decision flows in Figure 3.6 to judge whether or not the pension fund management process is conducive to change. In later sections the ability of a pension fund management process cast in the form of Figure 3.6 to improve its economic efficiency as well as to change will be considered. Figure 3.6 also generates a ready checkoff list for an analysis of a functional organization chart.

1. *Are all feedback loops closed?* This requirement is a variant of the concept that managers should have the authority to make decisions for which they are held responsible.

2. *Does the organization have adaptive or learning capabilities?* In order for this to be possible:
   a) Goals must be measurable.
   b) Feedback must be in goal and decision dimensions and be received in time to effect subsequent decisions.

3. *Is the system dynamically stable?* That is, are there procedures to dampen shocks to the system? In Cyert and March's framework, negotia-

38 / *A New Look at Portfolio Management*

Figure 3.6

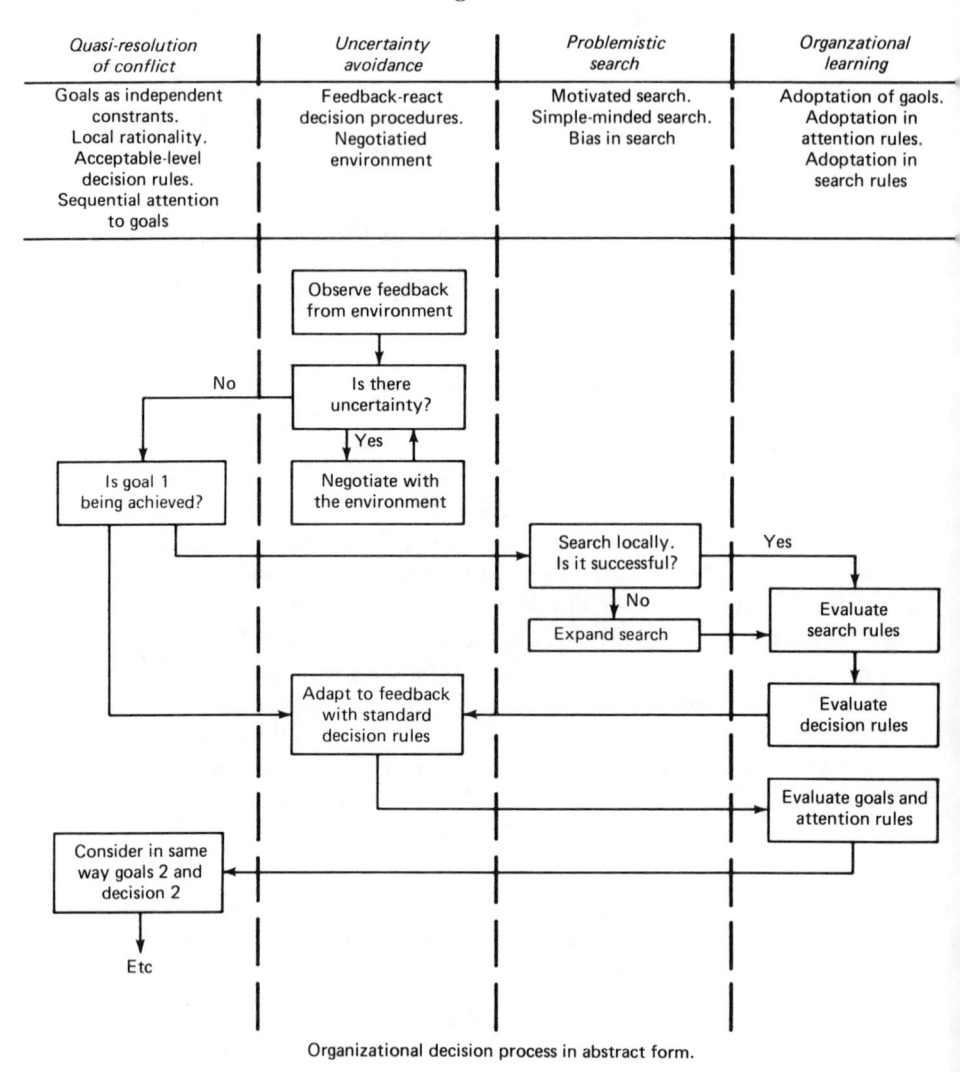

Quasi-resolution of conflict	Uncertainty avoidance	Problemistic search	Organzational learning
Goals as independent constraints. Local rationality. Acceptable-level decision rules. Sequential attention to goals	Feedback-react decision procedures. Negotiatied environment	Motivated search. Simple-minded search. Bias in search	Adoptation of gaols. Adoptation in attention rules. Adoptation in search rules

Organizational decision process in abstract form.

*Cyert and March [27] page 126.

tion with the environment to reduce uncertainty and thereby the potential for shocks along with search for new decision rules supply dampening forces.

As the first step in a behavioral analysis this check-off list is applied to Figure 3.5.

Beginning with item 1, closed feedback loops, we can find several which are not closed. Incidentally, feedback loops may be closed but ineffective because of inconsistencies between goal and feedback dimensions mentioned in 2b above. This problem is examined in a later section. Open loops, for example, existed for Senior Management, the Investment Policy Committee, Economics Department, Traders, Brokers and the Trustor himself. In all these centers of decision-making authority, measurable feedback on performance impact is missing. This absence of structured and measurable feedback flows would make it difficult for each of these areas to conclude that its contribution to performance goals were not being achieved. In terms of Figure 3.6, therefore, any search for new decision-making rules, in spite of pressures to do so, would appear to be unlikely.

These areas might have, however, implicitly perceived their goals to be other than performance related. Senior management, for example, might have informally established its goals in terms of participation. Feedback in this case would have taken the form of analysis of the percentage of available time spent in pension trust meetings. Negative external feedback would have then very possibly resulted in an increase in the frequency and length of senior management reviews but would not have changed the functional decision processes. Similar examples can be constructed for the other centers of decision-making authority. The point to be made is that even though the pension fund management process shown in Figure 3.5 might have had closed feedback loops for Senior Management, etc., these loops would not have been performance oriented and changes made by the organization in response to negative feedback through such loops would have resulted in improved performance only by chance. Furthermore, if an improvement in performance happened even occasionally by chance to have followed, for example, an increase in senior management participation, Skinner [68], Feldman [34] and other behavioralists [22] would predict that increased senior management participation in response to lagging performance would quickly become a firmly established standard.

Continuing the analysis with check-list item 2, it is clear that the organization described in Figure 3.5 would have had great difficulty in adpating to new circumstances. Goals, for example, were frequently expressed in non-measurable terms. This can be seen by referring back to Farnum's statement of investment policy, "trustee is required to employ such diligence and such prudence in the care and management of trust property as in general prudent men of discretion and intelligence employ in their own affairs." Even when goals were qualified in quantitative terms, such qualifications were usually statements of past performance without guidelines on how to indentify similar trends in the future. One large bank stated in 1972, the following in its internal "Investment Policy" statement:

> ... , we continue to emphasize high quality companies which have demonstrated an ability to produce above average earnings results.

On the other hand, in several institutions goals were expressed in terms such as "X percent more than the DOW." While this is certainly measurable and in the right direction to support an adaptive organization approach, the pure return dimensions of this goal fail to take into account the following organizational factors. Decisions were made by portfolio managers in terms of buy and sell recommendations, not in terms of expected return relative to the DOW. Thus the match up of feedback and goal dimensions required by item 2b was not met. Although the various committees might well have been aware of this goal when setting buy or sell ratings, there was no procedure to assure a common forecast for the DOW. Nevertheless, even if this problem were overcome, the best guess recommendations in nominal buy-sell form provided no information to the portfolio manager on the down-side risks for which he was held responsible. Goals were not the only problem. The security analyst's job in Figure 3.5 was to forecast earnings and yet his feedback and evaluation were in terms of equal dollar performance reports. Should the report have appeared negative, he had at least three plausible defenses because of the failure of feedback and goal dimensions to match up. One, he could have said the P/E forecast by the Investment Research Policy Committee had been at fault, or two, the supporting economic or brokerage research inputs had been highly misleading. As a third defense, he could have cited the inappropriateness of the equal dollar measure, since it would have been highly unlikely that any actual funds would have had a similar composition. In the institutions covered by this study, neither earnings nor P/E estimates and, more importantly, the assumptions on which these forecasts had been based, were collected in a manner which would have permitted an analysis of any of the security analyst's three defenses.

Unfortunately, both the Investment Research and Investment Policy Committees were in a similar position to effect decisions and yet avoid substantive evaluation.

The portfolio manager, on the other hand, received unambiguous, if not risk-adjusted, performance results on a quarterly schedule. As Figure 3.5 illustrates, the trustor also received these results and used them to allocate funds among different institutions. It was and still is common for large funds to have six or more trustees. If the results were inadequate the portfolio manager could have legitimately blamed the process generating the buy-sell decisions, since his influence on the portfolio composition had been minimal. However legitimate, such an explanation would have been poorly received by the trustor, with repetitions culminating in lost business. Should this have occurred, the portfolio manager would have been held responsible, and due to inappropriate feedback the organization would not have been able to learn by its mistakes. For these reasons, Figure 3.5 has been labeled a "Security Analyst Directed Organization."

The other major variant of the pension fund management process is shown in Figure 3.7. Comparison with Figure 3.5 reveals the only difference to be the ability of the portfolio manager to submit his own recommendations to the Investment Policy Committee. The net effect of this addition was to shift the role of the security analyst to an advisory one, even though he might still remain nominally responsible for making recommendations. Since the feedback reports were not altered, if poor performance should have resulted the portfolio mangers, as before, could have faulted the security analyst. However if good performance had been the case, he could then have taken credit for it. Figure 3.7, therefore, is labeled "Portfolio Manager Directed Organization." Again, the loss to the organization was not so much an issue of credit or blame but the absence of constructive feedback to foster organizational development.

Item 3 on the check-list deals with stability of the system. Until the advent of external performance measurement pressures reviewed in Chapter 2, the pension fund management process was extremely stable and, consequently, immune to change. The organizational problems raised in the analysis of check-list items 1 and 2 all point to the great difficulty the process would have had in internally generating forces for change. In addition, the uncertainty avoidance involved in arriving at a single best guess earnings estimate to summarize a complex corporate analysis is consistent with similar stabilizing behavior observed by Cyert and March in many other corporations.

The uncertainty avoidance phenomena recognized by Cyert and March is reinforced by studies of the cognitive limits of the human mind. Miller

Figure 3.7

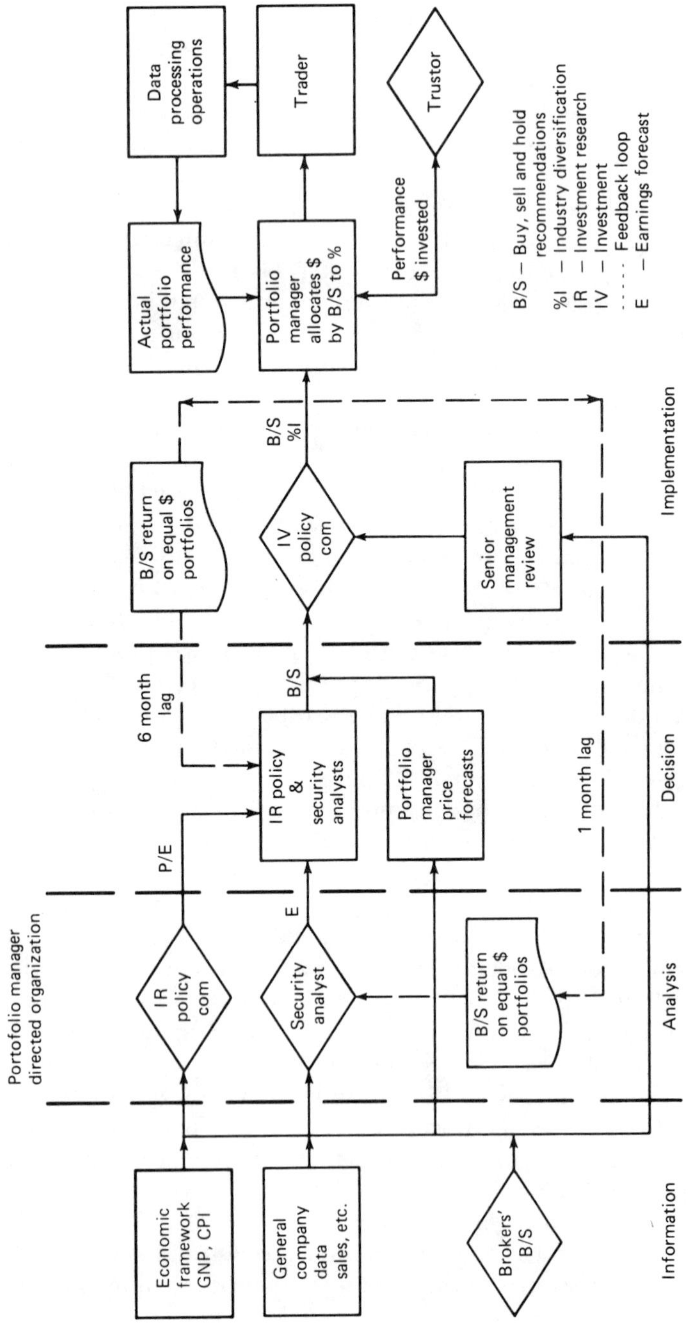

Portofolio manager directed organization
Economic framework GNP, CPI
General company data sales, etc.
Brokers' B/S
IR policy com
Security analyst
B/S return on equal $ portfolios
P/E
E
IR policy & security analysts
Portfolio manager price forecasts
6 month lag
1 month lag
B/S
B/S return on equal $ portfolios
IV policy com
Senior management review
B/S %I
Actual portfolio performance
Portfolio manager allocates $ by B/S to %
Performance $ invested
Data processing operations
Trader
Trustor
Information
Analysis
Decision
Implementation
B/S — Buy, sell and hold recommendations
%I — Industry diversification
IR — Investment research
IV — Investment
----- Feedback loop
E — Earnings forecast

[54], for example, discovered that the human mind is constrained to 7 ± 2 bits of information on a single input into memory. This cognitive limitation is certainly a major reason why the observed qualitative rankings used to communicate the relative attractiveness of a security usually contain five classifications, e.g. Sell, Neutral −, Neutral, Neutral +, Buy, and in the observations of the author, never contain more than nine. Thus even if pension fund managers did not try, in Cyert and March terms, "to negotiate with the environment to avoid uncertainty" their cognitive limitations would, nevertheless, have generated similar results.

The formal organization structures, reasonable on the surface in grouping similar activities, reinforced the behavioral inertia to change. Informal feedback among security analysts, portfolio managers and traders was discouraged by having them in different departments reporting to different managers and frequently in different physical locations as well.

Contrasted against these internal structures which made change difficult, developments in performance measurement took a form which made change inevitable. The thrust on the part of the performance measurers was not to negotiate away uncertainty, but to make it explicit and measurable. Goals in measurable form if not initiated by pension fund managers, were supplied to them by their customers. In short, during the late 1960's the pension fund industry was caught between strong external pressures for change and an internal structure unable to change. Cantor and Fiske blamed "size." But it should now be clear that growth in itself was not the problem, but only one of the factors which combined to disclose the real organization problems.

OFF-THE-SHELF MANAGEMENT SCIENCE

The fourth component of Leavitt's organizational change is technology or tools. By 1968, a substantial body of management science literature had developed on mathematical approaches to stock price forecasting and portfolio management. Could these tools have been used to breach some of the organizational barriers to change? Although a comprehensive review of this research is beyond the scope of this study,* the two following examples should provide an answer to this question.

Portfolio Selection

Markowitz's 1952 landmark paper [50] defined the portfolio selection

---

*See Elton and Gruber [29] for a recent collection of papers.

problem in mathematical terms, a subsequent paper in 1956 proposed an efficient algorithm to solve large scale problems [51] and IBM in 1962 [43] made this algorithm available on its 7000 series computers. The Markowitz algorithm was designed to select securities which would maximize portfolio return over the next period subject to a given level of risk measured by the expected variance of this return. Markowitz had been astute in recognizing that the variance of return for a common stock portfolio would be less than a sum of the individual variances unless all the stocks in the portfolio were perfectly correlated, a virtually impossible case. Thus his algorithm provided a mathematically rigorous method to combine quantitative estimates of future returns and covariances between these returns to determine just the right diversification mix for each optimal risk return combination. During 1970, the author made an informal survey of seven large institutions which accounted for over 50 percent of all pension funds. Not one was using the Markowitz algorithm or Sharpe's Beta model simplication [60] to manage pension funds nor were they aware of any institutions which were. One *Institutional Investor* article in September 1970, which reviewed the industry's use of computers in investment decision-making also fails to cite any actual applications, even though the conceptual influence is widely acknowledged. Why was this important new tool not used by pension fund managers? The answer to this question can be found in Figures 3.5 and 3.7 and is discussed below.

Qualitative Inputs

In Figure 3.5 the manager's input data was expressed in qualitative buy-sell terms. The Markowitz algorithm, however, requires quantitative estimates of returns and covariances. Hence, in this organization form the necessary data to drive the algorithm is absent. In Figure 3.7 it could have been argued that since the portfolio manager generated buy-sell decisions, he might have used this algorithm by converting his own inputs into the required quantitative format. There are several reasons why this would not have been possible. The portfolio manager as well as the security analyst was required to submit his recommendations to the Investment Policy Committee. Their decisions were expressed in buy-sell form and represented the official input to the portfolio management decision. Bypassing this step would not only have violated organization norms, but also the legal requirements set forth in Regulation 9.

It might be further argued that even so, the portfolio manager could still have used the algorithm and allowed the Committee to review his decisions for a possible overrule on an exception basis. Would this approach have encouraged the use of the Markowitz algorithm? The answer is, "probably no;" and its justification lies in a comparison of the risks actually faced by pension fund managers with those assumed by Markowitz.

Risk Assumptions

Markowitz's definition of risk is pictured in Figure 3.8. The curve labeled "Regret" indicates the square of the difference between the expected average return and all possible returns between plus and minus infinity. Hence Regret by the investor in Markowitz's framework is assumed to be zero if the actual return should happen to be $\bar{R}$ and grows quadratically as actual return differs in either direction from $\bar{R}$. Risk is computed via the calculus by summing all values of Regret between + and − infinity times the probability of each value. For example, in Figure 3.8, p · r would be a component of this sum. Markowitz was aware that investors do not usually regret doing better than average. He was quick to point out the normal probability curve he had assumed for expected returns was symmetric. Thus the risk above $\bar{R}$ would equal the risk below $\bar{R}$ and total risk, the sum of the two, would be just twice the downside risk from $\bar{R}$. He then went on to show that his algorithm produced the same portfolios whether total risk or one half of total risk was used. The advantage of using total risk is that it is equivalent to the statistician's variance and greatly simplifies the task of designing algorithms to determine portfolios. The disadvantage of using total risk or variance can be seen by referring to Figure 3.9. Even though it is almost certain, assuming normal probability distributions, that portfolio B will have a higher return than A, Markowitz's risk measure would classify B as much riskier than A. This anomaly was noted by Baumol in 1963 [16], and prompted him to consider a minimum return criteria to incorporate risk. In Chapter 4, it will be shown that Baumol's approach is much more relevant than Markowitz's to the risks actually faced by pension fund managers. The point to be made here, however, is that if a pension fund manager had a forecast of say 10 percent return for the market, A, not B as indicated by Markowitz, would be perceived as the risky portfolio. This conflict with the pension fund manager's operating definition of risk would make acceptance of portfolios generated by Markowitz's algorithm highly unlikely. Markowitz's use of variance to measure investment risk in general also needs to be examined in the specific context of fiduciary investment.

46 / *A New Look at Portfolio Management*

Figure 3.8

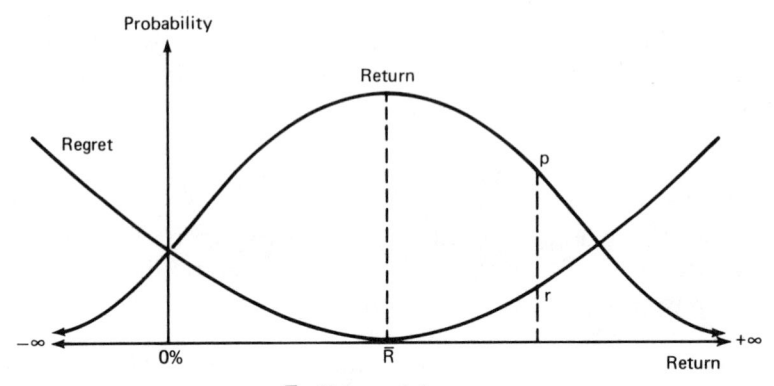

$\bar{R}$ = Mean portfolio return
$\tilde{R}$ = Random returns
Regret = $(\tilde{R} - \bar{R})^2$

Figure 3.9

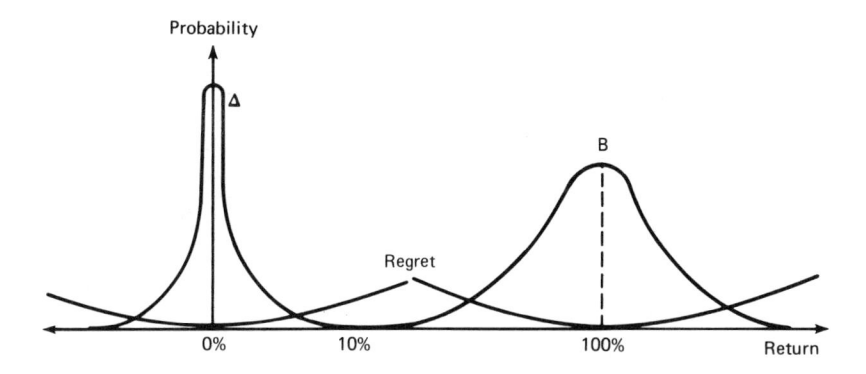

Initially, the assumption of normality and therefore symmetrically distributed returns cannot be valid since losses on securities purchased by pension funds are limited to the purchase price of these securities,* e.g. -100 percent and not $-\infty$ percent. Thus, variance computed as though returns were normally distributed would tend to overstate downside risk.

Secondly, the assumption of a quadratic Regret function centered about expected return does not describe accurately the actual Regret and Reward functions facing the pension fund manager. Although the exact form of these functions may be difficult to determine, all pension fund managers would expect to lose an account if they consistently underperformed the market or if they were always in the market when it would have been better to be in cash or short-term debt securities. In fact, under the Prudent Man concepts cited earlier, their firms might be sued as well as lose the account. From a personal viewpoint, the pension fund manager would not want to be in a shakey account situation since senior management in his firm, via the Investment Policy Committee, would usually get involved in an effort to save the account. Situations like this would do little to advance the manager's career. There is, therefore, great reluctance on the part of a pension fund manager to take risks which might result in below market or, in particular, negative returns. On the other hand, it is hard to establish how far above the market a portfolio manager must attain consistently to attract significant new business. Since few firms have formula bonus plans, it is even harder for him to estimate his own future salary gains related to this new business.

Thus the portfolio manager has tangible evidence on the costs to him of assuming too much downside risk and limited information on the benefits associated with higher opportunity risks. Figure 3.10 highlights this conflict, even when the location problem shown in Figure 3.9 is not a factor, between Markowitz's assumptions and the realities of pension fund management.

Other Considerations

Although the difficulties presented thus far should be more than enough to explain why Markowitz's algorithm has not been used for pension fund management, there are additional problems. Since these additional difficulties have, however, been covered by other researchers, the outline below has been included for completeness.

*This assumes that under Prudent Man Doctrine, the institution would not be liable for more than the actual decline. Even if additional punitive charges were assessed, they would be much nearer -100 percent than $-\infty$ percent.

Organizational Analysis / 49

Figure 3.10

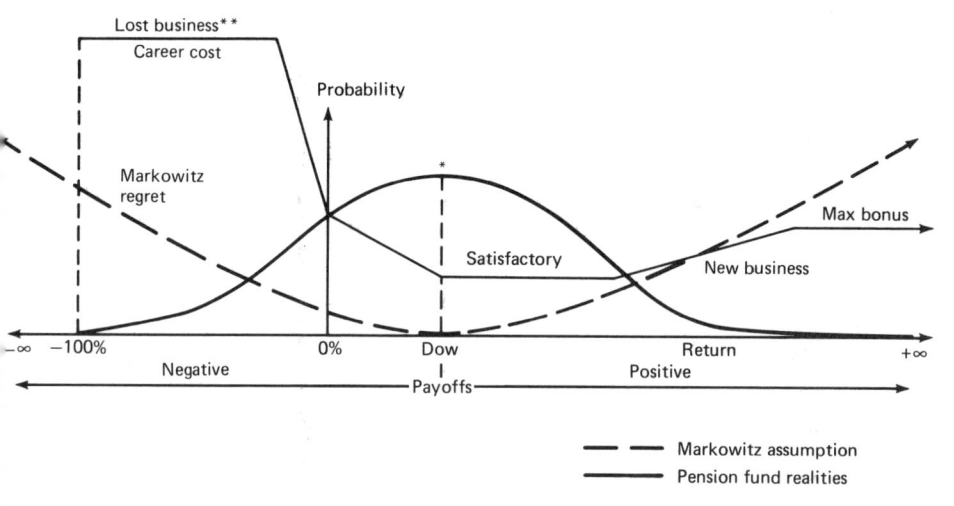

- - - Markowitz assumption
——— Pension fund realities

*The same expected return and variance is used for both measures of risk.
**The level of the pension fund manager's regret function will vary slightly with the size of the account, but not in direct proportion.

50 / *A New Look at Portfolio Management*

1. *Multi-period management vs single-period selection.*

The presence of transaction costs rules out the possibility of solving the long-term management problem by simply resolving Markowitz's algorithm each period. See Pogue [58], J. Smith [71] or K. Smith [72] for detailed treatments of this issue.

2. *Satisficing vs Optimizing.*

Simon [66] and other organizational researchers support the theory that managers do not optimize decisions, but stop in their efforts to solve problems when a satisfactory result is achieved. Hence many marginal decisions generated by a Markowitz algorithm in order to achieve optimum results could be perceived as unnecessary by management. This is consistent with Figure 3.10.

3. *Beta Instability.*

The instability of betas was discussed in Chapter 2 in relation to performance measurement. Sharpe's [60] simplification of the input required to execute the Markowitz algorithm could be an important breakthrough. Unfortunately it is based on perfect knowledge of the underlying alphas and betas for each security. Although historic instability does not rule out such forecasts, it clearly makes the task very difficult for analysts who are used to forecasting unconditional earnings or portfolio managers accustomed to a qualitative management style.

Security Evaluation Models

The second major area of research has been in the development of stock price forecasting models. Models by Malkiel [49], Gordon [41], Peck [79] and the author [4] are representative of the extensive work done in this area. Even though the latter two models were constructed within money management firms and demonstrated competitive performance, when compared to security analysts, their actual use was very limited. Neither have been in use since 1971, and the author has not been able to find any pension management firms which actively use such models in stock selection.

It is difficult to explain the failure of this new tool on the basis that it does not correspond to the problem perceived by the security analyst or portfolio manager. In fact, the model designed by the author is patterned on the way security analysts forecast earnings and P/E ratios [4].

There is, however, at least one plausible explanation. The absence of effective feedback loops in Figures 3.5 and 3.7, as discussed earlier, prevent management from making a substantive comparison of model vs analyst forecasts, as well as the analyst vs himself or other analysts. Given the strong safety-first philosophy necessary under Prudent Man regulations, it would be an unwise management decision to accept the recommendations of a computer model over those of an experienced analyst unless justified by rigorous statistical tests over a number of market cycles. To date, only three or four major institutions, including the one which provided data for this study, appear to have made the commitment to collect analysts' forecasts in a structured manner in order to be able to make these tests after a period of several years. In response to the initial question, "Could these tools have been used to breach some of the organizational barriers to change?", the answer seems to be "No." The reasons for this negative judgment can be traced to a basic conflict between assumptions underlying these tools and pension fund management realities, plus an inherent organizational barrier to new technology due to the absence of structured and effective feedback systems. In the next section, the steps which were taken at one major institution to structure its pension fund decision-making procedures are described. As a result of this effort, the institution was able to construct effective feedback loops and to generate the data necessary to evaluate the likely benefits of alternative approaches to pension fund management. It is this data upon which the tests in this study are conducted.

STRUCTURED-DECISION MAKING

Structured Decision-Making or SDM as it came to be known in the institution in which it was implemented, was a project initiated by the author to remove the organizational barriers to change. Although a complete discussion of the management process by which SDM was made a reality, the management education sessions, dedication of Management Science staff, professional faith of trust management, etc., is a very interesting story of organization change, telling the story of how SDM was implemented is beyond the scope of this study. The SDM system concept, however, is a critical bridge between pension management systems of the past and those of the future. Its structure provides tools to breach the barriers of organizational change and its operation over a period of years provided the data to examine in Chapter 5 the benefits and costs of alternative approaches to pension fund management.

Figure 3.11 illustrates the SDM system. Comparison with Figures 3.4 and 3.5 will show that SDM was an evolutionary step. All external information inputs were the same as shown in Figure 3.5 and the management system was still composed of the same organization groups. In fact, the

52 / *A New Look at Portfolio Management*

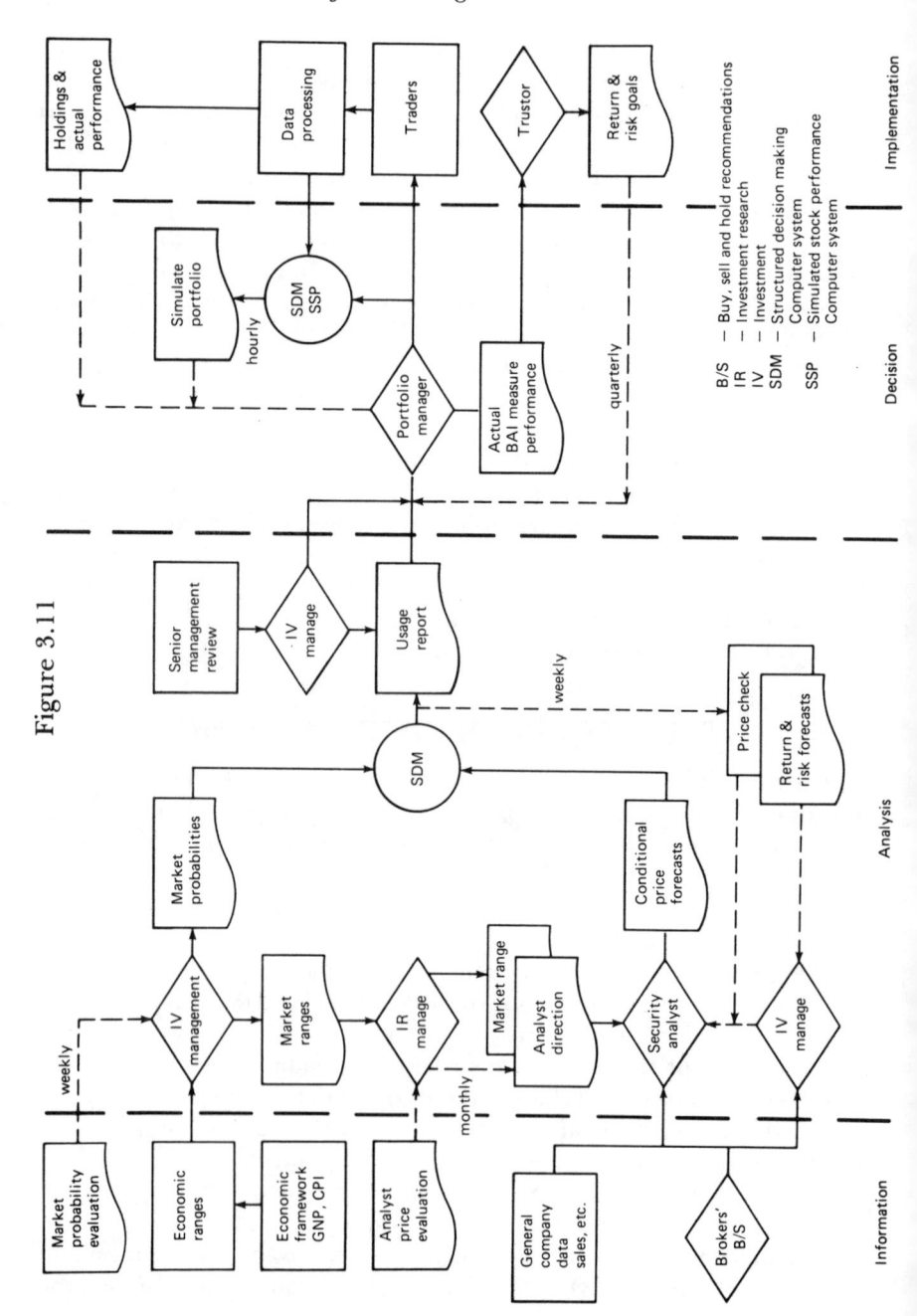

Figure 3.11

formal organization chart remained unaltered after SDM was installed. Important changes were made, however, to the functional or internal decision-making structure. These changes in terms of new tools, reports and responsibilities are discussed in the following sections.

Information

There are three new reports in the information phase of the system. Two of these are feedback reports, as indicated by the dashed lines, and will be reviewed later after the reports for which they provide feedback are introduced. This exposition difficulty is actually a good sign, since it is indicative of the closed loop nature of the new system.

The third new input is entitled "Economic Ranges" and is an expanded version of the "Economic Framework" in Figure 3.5. Its purpose is to enable the economists who support the pension management effort to elaborate in written form on the full range of possible economic environments over the next year. This is in contrast to the verbal best guess scenario they had provided under the old system. Economic alternatives are defined in terms such as GNP, Industrial Production, Consumer Prices, etc., and are assigned probabilities.

Analysis

Investment Management, the Investment Policy Committee in Figure 3.5, translates the Economic Range inputs into three mutually exclusive environments for the equity markets characterized by ranges and associated probabilities for the Dow Jones Industrial Index. Figure 3.12 is a sample of the combined Market Ranges and Market Probability reports.* Investment Research Management, the Investment Research Policy Committee in Figure 3.5, dicusses with the security analysts the implications of each market range and the corresponding economic conditions for their industries and companies.

The Analyst Direction report is based on a statistical analysis of past forecasting errors made by each analyst for every company he follows. If, for example, the Analyst Price Evaluation report indicated that an analyst consistently estimated future price appreciation too high, he would be encouraged to review his next forecast for any unjustified optimism.

---

* The date of this report has been removed in the spirit of retaining as much anonymity as possible for the participating institutions. Consistent with this policy, certain reports, such as internal performance evaluations, which are not directly relevant to the generation of data used in this study will be described but not shown.

54 / *A New Look at Portfolio Management*

Figure 3.12.

Forecasted Market Environment

DJIA . . . 625-1000   DJI 71-EARN . . . 53.0   DJI DIVD . . . 32.4
(Forecast Revised)

MARKET 1	MARKET 2	MARKET 3
Price 625-775	Price 775- 875	Price 875-1000
P/E 11.8-14.6	P/E 14.6-16.5	P/E 16.5-18.9

Implicit Market Returns

Based upon a current market level of 876.2, the following returns are possible from an investment in the Dow Jones Industrial Average over the next year:

MARKET 1	MARKET 2	MARKET 3
Range-25.0 –7.9%	–7.9 3.6%	3.6 17.8%
Exp Ret–16.4%	–2.1%	10.7%

Overall (Weights = .15   .50   .35)

Exp Dow Price = 846   Exp Dow Return = 0.21%

The security analyst, having researched each of his companies and having received the market and feedback information from his management, is now in a position to make his forecasts. The form of these forecasts, however, is very different from the qualitative recommendations he used to make and is the key to the SDM system. The analyst forecasts, conditional on each market range a low, most likely, and high price for each of his companies twelve months in the future. He also forecasts the average dividend he expects to prevail over the next twelve months. These forecasts are updated on a weekly basis and provide the data for the Conditional Price report. A copy of a page from this report is shown in Figure 3.13.

The initial reports from the SDM computer system are feedback reports to the analysts and management. Figure 3.14 is the Return and Risk feedback report corresponding to the conditional price forecasts in Figure 3.13.

Prior to discussing this report, it is important to clarify the assumptions behind it. The low, most likely, and high estimates are assumed to define a triangular probability distribution.* The distributions defined by the estimates for Boeing in Figure 3.13 are given in Figure 3.15. It is apparent that unlike the normal distribution assumed by Markowitz, the triangular distribution need not be symmetric nor need it extend to plus and minus infinity. This flexibility, for example, permitted the Boeing analyst to reflect his increasing optimism as the market scenario improved without letting his best guess or most likely estimates go above $20. Although the mathematical details of this distribution are treated in Chapter 4, it is useful at this point to note that its expected value can be found by simply averaging the three parameters. The expected price in the low market, therefore, is computed by:

$$\frac{12 + 15 + 17}{3} = \$14.67$$

If we add to this the expected dividend of $.40, then the expected percent return, given a current price of $25.00, is computed by:

$$\frac{14.67 + .40 - 25.00}{25.00} = -39\%$$

---

* See Chapter 4, the section entitled Security Return, for a mathematical definition of the triangular distribution and its relevant properties.

56 / *A New Look at Portfolio Management*

Figure 3.13

Forecasted Prices

Company Name	Current Price	Low Market Low	Low Market Most Likely	Low Market High	Middle Market Low	Middle Market Most Likely	Middle Market High	High Market Low	High Market Most Likely	High Market Highly	Div
Aerospace											
Boeing	25.	12.	15.	17.	16.	20.	25.	18.	20.	30.	0.40
Gen Dynamics	29.	15.	20.	25.	18.	25.	30.	20.	30.	35.	0.0
Grumman	20.	11.	14.	16.	13.	17.	18.	15.	19.	25.	1.00
Martin Marietta	22.	15.	20.	25.	18.	24.	27.	20.	30.	32.	1.10
Mc Donnell Douglas	39.	25.	30.	35.	28.	35.	45.	35.	45.	65.	0.39
North Amer Rockwell	35.	18.	22.	26.	25.	33.	35.	25.	36.	45.	1.40
United Aircraft	35.	20.	24.	40.	30.	45.	50.	35.	50.	60.	1.80
Air Transport											
Amer Airlines	43.	30.	35.	40.	40.	52.	60.	50.	60.	70.	0.0
Braniff Airway, Inc	17.	13.	17.	21.	18.	21.	26.	22.	26.	32.	0.0
Cont Airlines	23.	15.	20.	25.	20.	28.	33.	28.	34.	42.	0.0
Delta Air Lines	54.	35.	45.	50.	50.	60.	70.	60.	70.	80.	0.50
Eastern Air Lines	25.	10.	15.	20.	18.	28.	35.	28.	35.	45.	0.0
National Airlines	38.	20.	25.	30.	28.	38.	45.	38.	45.	60.	0.0
Northwest Airlines	43.	25.	30.	35.	38.	45.	55.	45.	55.	65.	0.45
Pan Am World Airways	15.	10.	15.	20.	10.	25.	30.	10.	30.	40.	0.0
Trans World Airlines	50.	25.	35.	45.	45.	60.	70.	60.	70.	85.	0.0
UAL	44.	30.	40.	50.	50.	55.	65.	55.	65.	75.	0.0
Automotive											
Chrysler	32.	21.	25.	29.	30.	36.	42.	36.	42.	50.	0.60
Cummins Engine	58.	33.	36.	43.	43.	60.	73.	53.	72.	87.	0.88
Ford Motor	73.	68.	74.	78.	76.	90.	96.	83.	99.	106.	2.60
General Motors	80.	80.	86.	92.	90.	109.	120.	100.	120.	130.	4.25
Libbey-Owens-Ford	47.	39.	46.	55.	46.	62.	70.	61.	78.	89.	2.00
Bank											
BankAmerica	71.	55.	62.	70.	62.	72.	80.	70.	80.	88.	1.55

Organizational Analysis / 57

Return Forecasts

Company Name	Market 1: Low Exp % Return	Market 1: Low 50–50 Range	Market 2: Middle Mkt Loss Prob	Market 2: Middle Exp % Return	Market 2: Middle 50–50 Range	Market 3: High Mkt Loss Prob	Market 3: High Exp % Return	Market 3: High 50–50 Range	Mkt Loss Prob	Overall Range
Aerospace										
Boeing	−39	−42 −36	100	−16	−21 −11	100	−6	−15 1	100	−50 24
Gen Dynamics	−30	−36 −25	100	−15	−22 −9	100	−1	−9 7	100	−48 22
Grumman	−25	−29 −21	100	−13	−17 −9	100	5	−2 13	99	−39 33
Martin Marietta	−2	−9 4	39	11	5 18	57	32	23 41	50	−26 53
McDonnell Douglas	−21	−25 −18	99	−6	−12 1	96	26	14 38	67	−34 69
North Amer Rockwell	−33	−36 −30	100	−7	−12 −2	100	5	−3 14	99	−44 33
United Aircraft	−16	−26 −7	78	22	14 32	27	41	31 52	30	−39 74
Air Transport										
Amer Airlines	−20	−23 −16	99	17	10 23	41	38	31 45	33	−31 61
Braniff Airway, Inc	2	−5 9	25	30	23 37	8	60	51 67	1	−22 93
Cont Airlines	−14	−20 −8	79	16	8 25	42	49	40 58	12	−36 81
Delta Air Lines	−20	−24 −15	98	11	6 16	61	29	24 35	66	−35 48
Eastern Air Lines	−41	−47 −35	100	6	−3 16	67	42	32 52	29	−61 77
National Airlines	−35	−39 −31	100	−3	−10 3	94	25	16 33	74	−48 57
Northwest Airlines	−28	−32 −25	100	9	3 15	67	31	24 37	59	−40 54
Pan Am World Airways	−1	−11 9	38	43	23 65	18	76	47 107	17	−34 165
Trans World Airlines	−30	−36 −24	100	17	9 24	40	43	36 51	20	−50 70
UAL	−9	−16 −2	63	29	24 34	6	48	41 54	9	−32 71
Automotive										
Chrysler	−19	−23 −16	98	15	10 21	45	36	30 43	40	−32 59
Cummins Engine	−34	−37 −32	100	3	−5 10	81	23	15 32	76	−42 52
Ford Motors	4	2 6	3	24	20 28	14	36	31 41	38	−3 49
General Motors	13	11 15	0	38	33 44	1	51	46 57	3	6 68
Libby-Owens-Ford	4	−1 9	14	31	24 39	9	67	58 76	0	−12 95
Bank										
BankAmerica	−10	−13 −7	74	3	−1 7	90	14	10 10	100	−20 26

This same result can also be found in Figure 3.14 by referring to the EXP% RETURN in MARKET 1 LOW for Boeing. The 50-50 RANGE of −42% to −36% states that, given the triangular distribution formed from the analysts' estimates for the low market, there is a 25 percent chance returns will be below −42%, a 25 percent chance it will be above −36% and a 50 percent chance it will fall in between. The distribution is pictured in Figure 3.16.

A further simplifying assumption is made in SDM of the independence within a market environment between market and stock returns. In the context of Figure 3.16, if the market turned out to be at its lowest possible anticipated return of −9%, this would provide no information on what value between −50% and −30% Boeing might have returned. In the case of Boeing, however, this assumption is not needed to compute the probability that Boeing returns will be below market returns. From Figure 3.16 this probability is clearly 100 percent for the low market. Again, the same result is given in Figure 3.14 for Boeing. The purpose of the expected return, 50-50 range and market loss probabilities is to generate feedback to the analyst on the implications of his forecasts and to supply this information in dimensions different from his original low, most likely and high estimates. Slovic (69), in reviewing this issue makes the following statement:

> For example, a financial analyst who is forecasting a stock's market price six months hence might be led to overweigh previous price information, simply because of the compatability factor. And if he were asked to forecast percentage price increase rather than price itself, he might give more weight to other variables in the company report that were expressed in terms of percentages.

The feedback approach in SDM is designed to minimize any compatibility biases.

If, for example, the −39% seemed "too low" or if the analyst felt he needed better odds than 50-50 to bet that return would, given a low market, fall between −42% and −36%, he might revise his original price estimates upward and spread them out a little more as well. This revision process would continue until the analyst was satisfied with both his price estimates and their implications. SDM, in this way, facilitates a repeated and convergent sampling of the analysts' subjective beliefs concerning future price performance conditional on a particular market environment. The Price Check Report is an analysis of the overlap in price ranges between adjacent markets. Referring to Figure 3.13, if the Chrysler

Figure 3.15. Conditional Price Forecasts for Boeing Aircraft

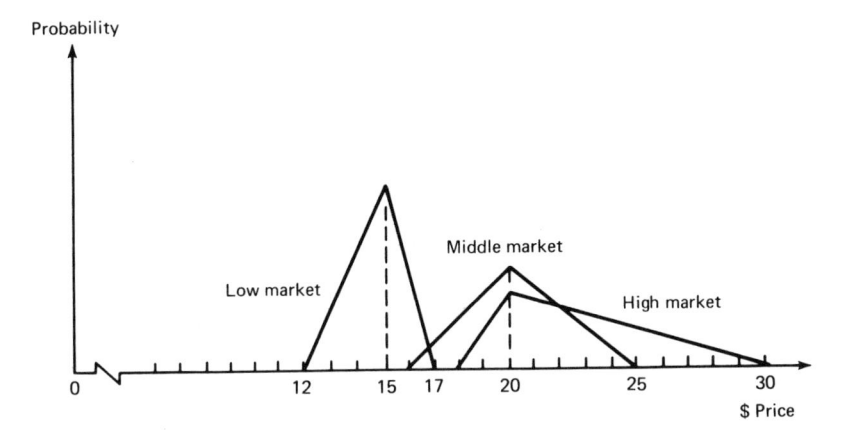

60 / *A New Look at Portfolio Management*

Figure 3.16. Conditional Return Forecasts

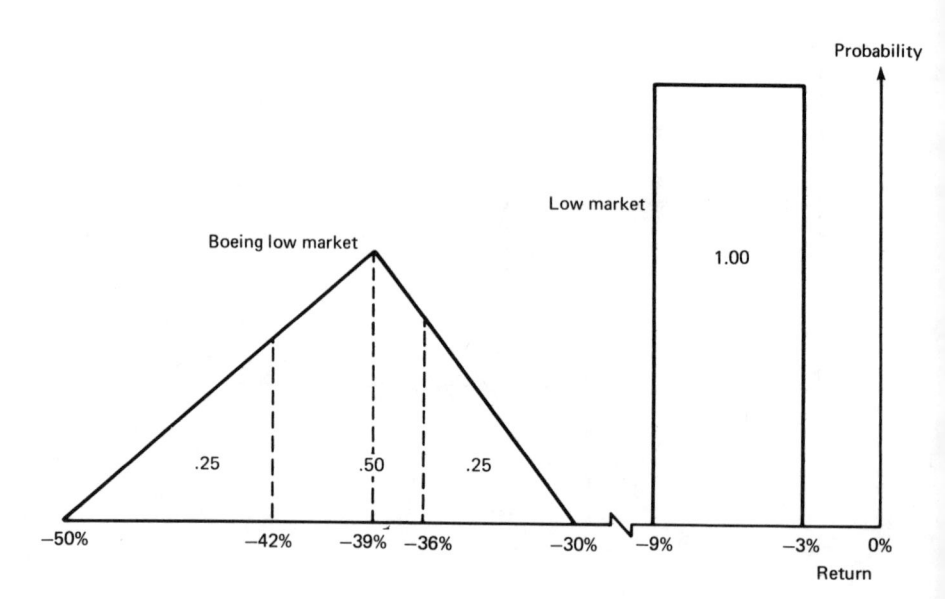

analyst had forecasted a high of $28 instead of $29 for the low market, then according to the probability assumptions, it would have been impossible for Chrysler to sell for $29. This feedback report identifies such unlikely gaps. While the analysts are translating their research into conditional price estimates, the management of the Investment Department translates its valuation of the macroeconomic situations into probabilities for the three mutually exclusive market environments. When the analysts' feedback cycle is complete, the SDM computer system produces the Usage Report. A page from this report is shown in Figure 3.17. This report combines the expected returns in each market with the market probabilities at the top of the report into an overall expected return. The overall expected return for Boeing is computed by:

$$.2(-39\%) + .7(-16\%) + .1(-6\%) = -19\%$$

and is given as value for Boeing in the Usage Report.

This report also introduces the concept of expected gain or loss. In Figure 3.18 both stocks A and B would have a 100 percent probability of being below the market. This probability alone, however, would clearly be misleading since A also has a 100 percent chance of falling below B. The Loss line, which measures how far each possible return is below the market return, when multiplied times the probability of each possible return gives a more representative measure—the expected loss. Both Boeing and General Dynamics, for example, have in Figure 3.14 a 100 percent chance of falling below the market. Boeing, however, is generally lower in all markets. This is reflected in the overall expected loss figures of 31.4% for Boeing vs. 28.9% for General Dynamics. The concept of expected gain is the mirror image of expected loss and represents the opportunity to outperform the market. Senior and Investment Management play a similar review and responsibility role, but they now have access to the assumptions and forecasts of the security analysts prior to any effort to classify stocks as buy, sell or hold.

Decision

In SDM the working document for the portfolio manager is the Usage Report. He is now responsible, given the needs of each Trustor, for determining which stocks should be bought and sold. The Usage Report supplies him with his downside risk in expected loss terms if he buys or holds a security, and with his opportunity risk if he sells or fails to buy. It also provides him with the overall or unconditional expected return to

62 / *A New Look at Portfolio Management*

Figure 3.17
Stock Investment Report MKT WEIGHTS= 20% 70% 10%
(Usage Report)

	Company Name	--Over all Mkts-- Exp % Ret	Exp Loss	Cur Price	--Exp % Ret-- Mkt1	Mkt2	Mkt3	------Relative to Market------ --Exp Loss-- Mkt1	Mkt2	Mkt3	Mkt1	--Exp Gain-- Mkt2	Mkt3
361	Maytag	−9	21.2	43	−17	−8	0	12	22	33	0	0	0
*362	Hercules	−9	21.2	56	−23	−8	11	17	22	22	0	0	0
363	AMP	−9	21.2	75	−19	−8	4	14	22	29	0	0	0
364	Joy MFG	−10	21.6	71	−20	−8	0	14	22	33	0	0	0
365	Sperry Rand	−11	23.4	37	−39	−10	38	33	24	3	0	0	0
366	Sunbeam	−11	22.8	33	−23	−9	1	18	23	32	0	0	0
367	First Natl City	−11	22.7	47	−22	−10	1	16	23	32	0	0	0
368	Walker, Hiram	−11	22.9	46	−17	−11	−1	12	24	34	0	0	0
369	North Amer Rockwell	−11	22.9	35	−33	−7	5	27	21	28	0	0	0
370	Coca-Cola	−11	23.1	123	−23	−10	−1	17	23	34	0	0	0
371	Texas Instruments	−11	23.3	136	−30	−9	6	24	23	27	0	0	0
372	Marriott	−12	24.0	64	−26	−10	2	21	24	31	0	0	0
373	Boise Cascade	−12	24.9	20	−39	−9	15	34	23	19	0	1	1
374	Green Giant	−13	24.9	27	−26	−11	1	21	25	32	0	0	0
*375	Syntex	−13	25.1	86	−30	−10	1	24	24	32	0	0	0
376	AMF, Inc	−14	25.5	57	−30	−10	−5	24	24	38	0	0	0
377	Grumman	−14	25.8	20	−25	−13	5	20	27	28	0	0	0
*378	Rohm & Haas	−14	26.2	139	−29	−13	3	23	26	30	0	0	0
379	Upjohn	−14	26.2	76	−28	−12	−3	22	26	36	0	0	0
380	Amerada-Hess	−15	26.5	44	−30	−12	−1	24	26	34	0	0	0
381	Perkin-Elmer	−15	26.9	60	−32	−12	−3	27	26	37	0	0	0
*382	Air Products & Chem	−16	28.4	62	−29	−16	3	24	29	31	0	0	0
383	Intl Flavors & Frag	−17	28.5	56	−28	−16	1	22	30	33	0	0	0
384	Hewlett-Packard	−17	28.5	50	−39	−14	6	33	27	27	0	0	0
385	Gen Dynamics	−17	28.9	29	−30	−15	−1	25	29	35	0	0	0
386	Natl Cash Register	−17	29.4	34	−39	−14	0	34	28	33	0	0	0
387	Becton, Dickinson	−19	30.5	42	−27	−18	−8	21	32	41	0	0	0
388	Boeing	−19	31.4	25	−39	−16	−6	33	30	39	0	0	0
389	Dist Corp-Seagrams	−22	33.7	35	−29	−21	−13	24	35	46	0	0	0
390	Brunswick Corp	−22	33.7	44	−40	−20	1	35	34	33	0	0	0
391	Amer Standard	−22	35.4	16	−61	−18	25	55	32	15	0	0	7

weigh against his relative values for loss and gain risk. Although the Usage Report can be very valuable to a portfolio manager on a one stock at a time basis, and therefore an aid in following the Prudent Man philosophy, it could easily mislead him when considering the portfolio as a whole. In Figure 3.18 securities C and D have the same triangular distribution and therefore the same expected gain and loss. If C and D are different securities, then it is reasonable to assume they are not perfectly correlated with each other. If we construct a portfolio composed of 1/2C and 1/2D, it will have the same expected return—in this example equal to the market return—but lower expected gain and loss than either C or D. In short, while the return for a portfolio is equal to a weighted average of the component stock returns, a similar weighted average of the risks for each security would overstate the risks for the portfolio. Figure 3.19 illustrates how the probability distribution of a portfolio of C and D differs from the distribution of either one separately. The mathematics required to compute the expected gain and loss for a portfolio is complicated and does not lend itself to a tabular report format. Consequently, the SDM system includes an online computer terminal facility which permits the portfolio manager to evaluate the effect on expected portfolio return, loss and gain due to changes in portfolio composition. In Figure 3.11 this part of the system is shown by SSP which represents Simulated Stock Performance.

Implementation

The one change in this component was made by the institution's customers. Virtually all of the major accounts subscribed to A. G. Becker's Retirement Funds Evaluation Service [3]. A. G. Becker defines the "key elements" of their approach as:

measurement of rates of return earned on total fund assets and the principal asset components of the total fund;

comparison of these rates of return with rates of return earned by other funds of similar asset size and the total population as well;

evaluation of the factors which contribute to differences in performance among retirement fund assets.

The last element includes risk measures as defined by Treynor, Sharpe and Jensen.

64 / *A New Look at Portfolio Management*

Figure 3.18. Expected Gain and Loss

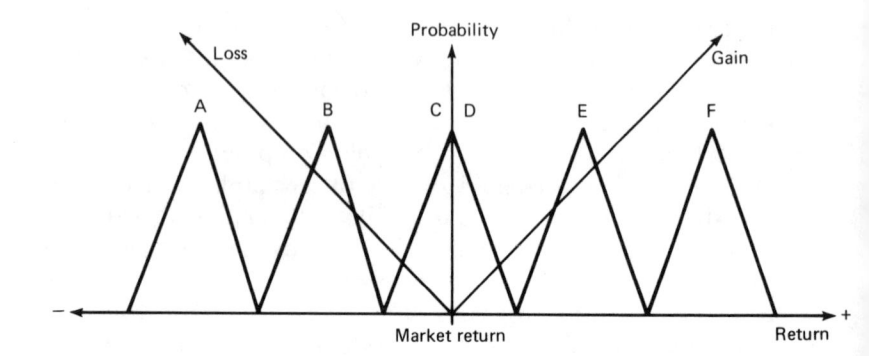

Figure 3.19. Diversification effects

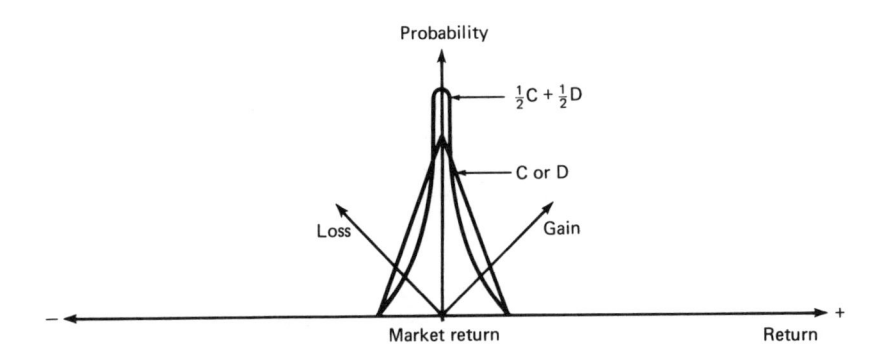

***Information**—Feedback Reports*

SDM had been in operation for approximately two years before the internal performance evaluation reports shown in the Information component were introduced. The initial year was simply the delay between making the forecasts and their realization. The second year was used to begin developing statistics on forecasting performance.

The function of the Market Probability Evaluation Report is to give Investment Management feedback on its ability to assign probabilities to market ranges. If, for example, given the management forecasts at the top of Figure 3.17, the middle market did occur twelve months later, the management score according to SDM would be 74 percent out of 100 percent maximum. On the other hand, if the high market had occurred, their score would have been only 18 percent. The central feature of the Analyst Price Evaluation Report is that the analyst is only evaluated in the market which actually occurred. His conditional expected return for the market range is compared with the actual return and statistics which give the sign and magnitude as well as the likely variation in the analyst forecasting errors are generated by SDM.*

SDM AND ORGANIZATIONAL CHANGE

Did the SDM effort remove any organizational barriers to change? Since the organization adopted the SDM approach and thereby made fundamental changes in its management style the answer must be, "Yes." In fact, the Trust Department conducted a national advertising campaign featuring the SDM concepts and the institution included a copy of this advertisement in its 1972 annual report. Several excerpts from this advertisement are reproduced below.

You won't find a cumbersome decision-making process at ———.

---

* The mathematics of this calculation is based on a comparison of the actual forecast with a perfect forecast. If a middle market had occurred, the perfect forecast would have been 0, 1, 0 with probability 1 for the middle market and probability 0 for the low and high markets. The score is then computed by

$$1 - \sqrt{((.2 - 0)^2 + (.7 - 1.)^2 + (.1 - 0)^2)}/\sqrt{2} = .74.$$

Several years ago, we decided that, in the changed investment environment, the traditional bank organization was not providing fast and flexible decisions on our accounts. So we took what was a very *un*bankish step at that time. Individual money managers were given investment responsibility and evaluated on their investment performance.

To check on the accuracy of the analysts' projections and to help plan portfolio strategy and stock selection, our management science group developed a computer technique called Simulated Stock Performance. Under varying economic forecasts, it ranks each stock by investment attraction and risk relative to the other securities we follow.

On a more fundamental level, and in the context of the Cyert and March framework, the primary barriers to organizational change removed by SDM are outlined below.

Closed Feedback Loops

Security analysts are held responsible and evaluated on their price forecasting ability in the market which occurs. They are not responsible for predicting market levels nor are they able to make implicit risk return tradeoffs in determining buys and sells. Portfolio managers receive forecasts and risk measures which permit them to tailor risk-return tradeoffs to specific Trustor needs. Management determines the degree to which the institution will bet on any market level and is accordingly evaluated in their ability to make this judgment.

Organizational Learning Capabilities

Organizational learning is greatly enhanced by having measurable return goals and risk constraints and by matching the dimensions in which decisions are made with the feedback on these decisions. Organizational learning also took place in a more literal sense. Security analysts and portfolio managers learned about concepts in statistics and decision theory and had the opportunity to use them daily.

Figure 3.20 is an example from the installation phase of SDM of how information which would have been lost or confused in a qualitative ranking system was obtained. Stocks A, B, C and D had all been rated N for Neutral or Hold. Stocks E and F had been rated F for Favorable and selected as Buys. Price forecasts, in the SDM format shown in Figure 3.13, were also supplied at the same time by the same analysts and used to compute the return percentages. A scan of the data reveals that stock D is

68 / *A New Look at Portfolio Management*

Figure 3.20

Expected Market	Down Market worst	Down Market most likely	Down Market best	Level Market worst	Level Market most likely	Level Market best	Up Market worst	Up Market most likely	Up Market best	Relative Stk Sig.
A	−36.51%	−4.93%	5.60%	−25.98%	5.60%	16.13%	−15.45%	16.13%	26.65%	N
B	−7.86%	0.18%	14.25%	−2.83%	14.25%	22.29%	2.19%	22.29%	32.34%	N
C	−11.32%	1.84%	15.00%	1.84%	8.42%	21.58%	1.84%	21.58%	28.16%	N
D	−0.76%	4.95%	8.76%	8.76%	14.48%	22.10%	18.29%	24.00%	33.52%	N

	Down Market worst	Down Market most likely	Down Market best	Level Market worst	Level Market most likely	Level Market best	Up Market worst	Up Market most likely	Up Market best	
E	8.06%	22.45%	36.84%	15.25%	36.84%	58.42%	29.64%	51.22%	72.81%	F
F	−24.48%	−16.36%	16.36%	−8.24%	3.94%	24.24%	3.94%	24.24%	44.54%	F

perceived to be always better than A, even though both are nominally ranked the same. In fact D would also appear to be a much better buy than F, even though the latter is rated as a buy and D is not.

Organizational Stability

Cyert and March [27] point out that firms "avoid uncertainty" at almost all costs. In fund management this avoidance takes the form of labeling a stock a "Buy" vs. forecasting the probability that the price will increase by X percent, or neglecting to keep records of recommendations which might increase the uncertainty about the validity of them.

As the incidence of uncertainty avoidance is reduced and as feedback loops are closed, the organization will become more dynamic and therefore less stable. No longer does the institution have to offer one investment image to facilitate internal control. As the price evaluation evidence builds up, analysts are unlikely to retain a consistent under or over estimation bias, but will alter their forecasts appropriately.

On the other hand, the organization might become dynamically unstable, swinging from one extreme to the other. This issue and many other normative questions about the revelance and desirability of the SDM approach will be tested empirically in Chapter 5.

Summary

In this Chapter the traditional pension fund management structures were examined in the context of Leavitt's components of organizational change. These structures were shown not to be conducive to change nor to the introduction of new decision-making technology. In addition, when off-the-shelf management science models were considered as a technological component of change, these models were shown to be inappropriate and therefore, ineffective in their present form. The SDM system which had been implemented in one large institution was introduced as an initial step toward making the organization structure more amenable to change. SDM is especially relevant to this study, since it was through this system that the forecasts used in the evaluation of alternative pension fund management systems in Chapter 5 were gathered.

Chapter 4

A General Pension Fund Management Simulator

During the implementation of the Structured Decision-Making system* it is stated in the Preface that, "the management of the Trust Department of the Bank, my staff and even our customers had faith that a better way of making decisions would necessarily generate better investment results." Many researchers, however, such as Ackoff [1] and Goldberg [40] have observed that more sophisticated tools or expanded information flows have not improved the quality of decisions. If, for example, analysts' forecasts are very poor, then fine-tuning portfolio decisions by using triangular distribution input instead of qualitative rankings could easily result in worse, not better, results. It is evident in the context of Leavitt's components of organizational change, that SDM did in fact effect change. It is also important to note that Leavitt's framework does not consider whether or not the performance of the organization was improved by this change.

Chapter 1 contains a discussion of why parallel testing of alternative management systems was not feasible. The basic research approach of this study, therefore, is to simulate alternative systems using the forecasts, structured in terms of both quantitative detail and controlled subjective sampling, gathered in SDM. If we accept that once forecasts are supplied by the analysts and goals of the trustor are established, the remaining task facing the portfolio manager can be reduced to a mathematical problem,

* Referred to subsequently as "SDM."

then a mathematical model could be used to simulate this facet of portfolio management. The appropriateness of the model would not depend on whether it produced optimal results, but on whether its investment decisions were at least as good as those which would have been produced by a portfolio manager working with the same data. If the model is constructed in a manner which does not incur the problems encountered by the off-the-shelf portfolio models, then this model could also be used to draw inferences about the performance of systems in which portfolio managers employed the model as a decision-making aid. In addition to these simulation requirements, the model must be general enough to represent all the alternative systems under examination if controlled, statistical evaluations are to be made. The purpose of this chapter is to develop a general pension fund management model which meets these requirements.

Although many of the following sections in this chapter are mathematical, the reader may without loss of continuity, skip the mathematical portions. For the reader who does wish to cover the mathematical portions, Appendix B provides a glossary of symbols. The managerially oriented reader should be able to acquire the main concepts in this chapter by first reading the summary at the end of this chapter and then scanning the sections, beginning with the following one.

OVERVIEW OF REPRESENTATIVE PORTFOLIO MANAGEMENT MODELS

The purpose of this study is the evaluation of alternative management systems and not the development of mathematical models for pension fund management. Consequently, the first step taken in the development of a general pension fund model was to review the history of portfolio management models to determine if any might be appropriate or easily modified.

There is a vast literature in this field stemming from Markowitz's 1952 paper. However, much of this literature is directed toward the theory of intertemporal utility maximization and is not directly translatable into operational pension management models. In order to focus this review, therefore, it is necessary to define the concept of "operational" in the context of pension fund management by a large institution. Part of this

72 / *A New Look at Portfolio Management*

definition has already been given in the critique of management science models in the last chapter. The model must be able to incorporate the safety-first aspect of Prudent Man risk. It must also be capable of using forecast data in the conditional distribution form generated in SDM. Additional facets of this concept beyond those introduced in Chapter 3 are outlined below.

Universe Size

The institution in which SDM was implemented had a list of stocks, suitable for prudent investment, which contained at a minimum 200 companies. Studies by Cohen and Pogue [25] have shown that for a given risk level, as measured by standard deviation of return, reducing the universe size also reduces the expected return. The model, therefore, should be able to handle at least 200 securities.

Universe Variation

A frequent critique of empirical work in portfolio management modeling is that only stocks which were acceptable investments for the entire simulation period are included in a fixed universe. In reality companies are delisted, new companies are added and prudent investment standards change. Failure to include, for example, a stock which because of corporate difficulties had fallen drastically had been liquidated by the institution during the simulation period, would cause a positive, pre-selection bias in the results. The model, therefore, should be able to operate with a fluctuating universe.

Portfolio Revision

Pension fund managers spend almost all of their time revising the composition of existing portfolios and very little time setting up completely new funds from initial cash contributions. Smith [72] has shown that single period models, such as the one proposed by Markowitz to set up a portfolio, are appropriate in a revision sense only if transaction costs are zero. Transaction costs are not zero, however, and include adverse market effects caused by the typically large transactions made by institutions as well as brokerage fees. The model, therefore, should consider these costs and be formulated to treat the revision problem.

Forecast Feedback

If security analysts supply forecasts of inconsistent and poor quality, portfolio managers would soon grow reluctant to act on them. This would occur even in cases such as the Structured Decision-Making system where the analysts have the opportunity to specify subjective forecasts variances if estimates turned out later to be unrepresentative of the true uncertainty in the forecasts. In order for the model to be operational, it must explicitly include feedback measures of the quality of the security analysts' forecasts and incorporate these measures into portfolio decision-making.

Number of Forecast Periods

The operational constraints of universe size, variation, feedback, safety and portfolio revision serve to complicate the modeling process. Some operational considerations, by restricting the generality of the problem, may actually simplify the modeling process. The first of these simplifying steps deals with the institutional and economic realities involved in forecasting an unconditional time series of prices for a particular security. Given the need to consider portfolio revision, the model must contain at least two periods, i.e. one to represent the current status and one to indicate portfolio composition after the changes are made. This would require only a single forecast of the security's price for one period ahead. In order to examine in detail the information requirements for a multi-period forecast, the forecasting problem facing the security analyst is structured below. The central idea underlying this anslysis is that the price of a security at any point in time is determined by the secondary equity market's balancing of current anticipations of future performance. If the analyst is to justify his recommendations, then he must be able to anticipate the market's anticipations better than the market itself.

As in (1)* a simple market model is assumed to explain security returns at any given point in time:

$$R - R_f = \alpha + \beta(R_m - R_f) \qquad (9)$$

*Equation (9) includes α, implying that certain non-systematic returns are available. In a long term equilibrium α would be zero. The analysis which follows is not dependent upon assumptions concerning the lever of α.

Using the definition of return in terms of price appreciation and dividends (9) can be rewritten as:

$$R_1 = \frac{P_1 + D_1 - P_0}{P_0} = R_{f,1} + \alpha_1 + \beta_1(R_{m,1} - R_{f,1})$$

where subscripts indicate time periods in the future from the current time which is indicated as 0.

Solving for P_0 gives:

$$P_0 = \frac{P_1 + D_1}{(1 + \alpha_1 + R_{f,1} + \beta_1(R_{m,1} - R_{f,1}))} = \frac{P_1 + D_1}{(1 + R_1)} \qquad (10)$$

All of the variables in (10), except $R_{f,1}$, are weighted estimates generated by the market equilibrium process at time 0. Restating (10) in terms of market estimates:

$$P_0^0 = \frac{P_1^0 + D_1^0}{(1 + R_1^0)} \qquad (11)$$

where a superscript identifies the variable as an estimate and the value of the superscript refers to when the variable is estimated. Further applications of this process yield the familiar present value formulation [78]:

$$P_t^j = \sum_{k=t+1}^{\infty} \frac{D_k^j}{\prod_{\ell=t+1}^{k}(1 + R_\ell^j)} \qquad (12)$$

where subscripts t, k and l indicate time periods from the present and j represents the period in which the overall marketplace arrives at its estimates for D_k and the components α_ℓ, $R_{f,\ell}$, β_ℓ and $R_{m,\ell}$ of R_ℓ. Although the market may not be in instantaneous equilibrium, e.g. $P_0 \neq P_0^0$, for the moment the assumption of equilibrium and therefore $P_0 = P_0^0$, will be made.

A General Pension Fund Management Simulator / 75

Initially, consider the task of forecasting just one period ahead. If action on this forecast is to generate an improvement in terms of the performance measures based on (9), then:

$$\hat{P}_1^0 \neq \hat{P}_1^1$$

where $\hat{P}_1^0$ is the analyst's current estimate of what the market currently forecasts the price to be one period ahead and $\hat{P}_1^1$ is his current estimate of the price one period ahead based on new market anticipations.

This task is clearly formidable. For example, since the variables in R_ℓ are all random variables, including R_f beyond the current period, he must be able to *estimate* how the market will *change* its *estimates* of these variables as well as their intertemporal covariances in order for him to compute $\hat{P}_1^0 - \hat{P}_1^1$.

Forecasting for two periods ahead is even more complex. Let v_ℓ^j represent any one of the following variables $\{D_\ell^j, \alpha_\ell^j, R_{f,\ell}^j, R_{m,\ell}^j, \beta_\ell^j\}$.
As the marketplace observes outcomes for these variables, learning theory would suggest that revisions of current anticipations would at a minimum be a function of observed forecasting errors and the time horizon of the estimate.

In algebraic terms:

$$v_\ell^j = \text{fct}_j(v_j - v_j^{j-1}, \ell) \tag{13}$$

or when $j = 1$ for input to a two period forecast:

$$v_\ell^1 = \text{fct}_1(v_1 - v_1^0, \ell) \tag{14}$$

Thus, the analyst, in order to determine whether or not $\hat{P}_2^0$ equaled $\hat{P}_2^2$ would have to estimate, in addition to all the anticipations required by the one period forecast, the recursive functions represented by (14) and future values for the observed variables in these functions.

When the assumption of market equilibrium is dropped, (12) can no longer be treated as an equality. To further complicate the problem, even *ex post* estimates of α_ℓ and β_ℓ frequently exhibit variances as large as the estimates themselves. Furthermore, forecasts of $R_{m,\ell}$ are recursive since $R_{m,\ell}$ is a function of individual security returns which in turn are functions of $R_{m,\ell}$.

The purpose of this section is to demonstrate that although analysts could be asked to make unconditional, multi-period price forecasts, the assumptions, ability and effort required to justify such a request would be extraordinary. Consequently, the models used to simulate pension fund management of equity securities can, in light of these observations, be realistically limited to considering just the current period, the interperiod flow and the next forecasted period for each conditional environment.

Limitations on Holdings

As mentioned in Chapter 2, Prudent Man legislation would preclude placing all funds in a single security, and portfolio managers are generally aware of the diversification benefits with even a dozen securities as shown by Sharpe. Short sales of securities are not viewed as prudent investments. Consequently, the management model should permit placing constraints on the maximum percentage of a fund invested in any one security and prohibit short sales of all securities.

Although these considerations may appear to make the problem more complex, they actually help to simplify it. The upper bound and short sale constraints facilitate approximating a linear programming solution with a simple ranking method. These constraints in combination with the central limit theorem also support the assumption of normality used later for the portfolios constructed.

Taxes

Since pension funds are not taxed, tax considerations are not included. This institutional fact greatly simplified the requirements, particularly the need to have multiple periods to incorporate tax carry forward and back situations.

Costs

The earlier constraints were directed toward identifying conditions under which an operational solution would be possible. Being able to solve the problem with a mathematical model, however, does not mean that it would necessarily be a worthwhile approach for pension management firms to follow.

Many institutions in the early 1970s discovered that their pension fund management efforts were at best generating modest profits. Markowitz's algorithm which does not include portfolio revision costs, could easily incur computer costs of several hundreds of dollars per run per account. Even those costs are likely to be minor in terms of the expense necessary to integrate the decision model into the institution's data processing system. Any model, therefore, if it is to be truly operational, should cost no more than a few dollars per run and must be easily intergratable into an ongoing data processing system for pension funds.

Review of Representative Models

A critical analysis of the appropriateness for pension fund management of all papers on portfolio management since Markowitz's key 1952 publication is well beyond the scope of this study. Seven important and representative proposals in addition to Markowitz's original formulation, however, are analyzed in Table 4.1 with regard to the operationality constraints.

Although Pogue's formulation appears to come closest to meeting these constraints, it is still critically deficient in the areas of risk definition, operating costs and the ability to be modularly incorporated into a pension fund accounting system. Pogue's formulation also suffers from an internal inconsistency which he recognized. Price forecasts are treated stochastically in the objective function, but deterministically in the cash flow constraints.

With the exception of modularity, each of the desired attributes is represented in at least one of the models. It is possible to combine, into one model, the low cost of Sharpe's Beta portfolio model,* with Baumol's risk approach and the advantages of Pogue's work? The author believes that it is indeed possible. The steps required to construct an operational model are presented in the remainder of this chapter.

In essence, the first step demonstrates how the *a priori* SDM forecasts can be transformed into nonlinear Beta models. Then Sharpe's diagonal framework is extended to a portfolio revision form with the inclusion of transaction costs and management fees. Approximation methods suggested by Stone [73] and Sharpe [63] are used to convert the quadratic

* See (1) page 20.

78 / *A New Look at Portfolio Management*

Table 4.1. Representative Portfolio Management Models*

Operational criteria \ Author	Markowitz [52]	Sharpe diagonal [63]	Sharpe beta [63]	Smith [72]	Glauber [39]	Chen, Jen, Zionts [23]	Baumol [16]	Pogue [58]
Safety first risk	N	N	N	N	N	N	Y	N
Conditional distribution input	Y	N	N	N	N	Y	Y	Y
Forecast feedback	N	N	N	N	N	N	N	Y
Revision and variation	N	N	N	Y	N	Y	N	Y
Transaction costs	N	N	N	Y	N	Y	N	Y
Percent limits and no short sales	Y	Y	Y	Y	N	Y	Y	Y
Computer codes for over 200 securities	Y	Y	Y	?	N	N	?	?
Low operating cost	N	N	Y	N	Y	N	N	N
Software modularity	N	N	N	N	N	N	N	N
Solution method	Quadratic programming	Quadratic programming	Ranking (linear prog.)	Quadratic programming	LaGrange multipliers	Dynamic programming	Quadratic programming	Quadratic programming

*Y - Yes
N - No

programming problem into a knapsack dynamic programming problem.** At this point, feedback correction to the SDM forecasts is also brought into play. Finally, a convergent approach is developed to estimate the knapsack solution which transforms it into a ranking problem which can be solved at very low cost. Throughout the development of this process, each step is designed to permit modular incorporation into pension data processing systems.

RISK FREE RETURN

The Beta model framework as well as the desire to provide for short term bond investment requires the use of a risk free bond rate. Since the revision frequency of the SDM data is one month, the three-month U.S. Treasury Bill rate 30 days prior to maturity has been selected as the risk free rate. This rate, however, is quoted on a 360-day discount, not on an annual dividend yield basis, and must be converted to be consistent with dividend yields on equity securities.

The discount is computed by:

$$d = \frac{360}{n}(\frac{100 - P}{P}) \qquad (15)$$

when n is the number of days to maturity, d is the quoted discount and P is the current market price.

The one month risk free rate is defined as:

$$R_f = (\frac{\text{Final Cash Value} - \text{Cost}}{\text{Cost}})\frac{365}{30} \qquad (16)$$

For a three-month Treasury Bill 30 days prior to maturity, (16) becomes:

$$R_f = (\frac{100 - P}{P})\frac{365}{30} \qquad (17)$$

** For the nontechnical reader, these are standard albeit expensive, mathematical techniques to solve portfolio composition problems.

Solving (15) for P and substituting into (17) results in:

$$R_f = .0845d \qquad (18)$$

MARKET RETURN

The Beta model framework also requires a forecast for market return. In SDM uniform, mutually exclusive distributions for market levels twelve months in the future along with the associated probability for each distribution are supplied monthly by management. In algebraic terms:

$$f(\tilde{I}_j | \text{Environment } j) = \begin{cases} \dfrac{1}{{}_H I_j - {}_L I_j} & {}_L I_j \leq \tilde{I}_j \leq {}_H I_j \\ 0 & \text{otherwise} \end{cases} \qquad (19)$$

where $\tilde{I}_j$ is the random outcome for the level of the index—in the case of SDM the Dow Jones—in Environment j, ${}_H I_j$ is the highest level possible in Environment j, ${}_L I_j$ is the lowest level possible and f is the conditional density function. Although the ranges for each environment are mutually exclusive, no gaps are permitted between ranges. Hence:

$$_H I_j = {}_L I_{j+1} \qquad (20)$$

In addition, all possible values for $\tilde{I}_j$ are assumed to be spanned by three specified environments and associated market ranges. Therefore:

$$\sum_{j=1}^{3} p_j = 1 \qquad (21)$$

where p_j is the probability that the jth environment will occur.

The assumption was also made by management that the dividend for the index is independent of the environment and can be estimated for the next twelve months by using the actual dividend over the last twelve months.

Market return $\tilde{r}_{m,j}$ can be computed by:

$$\tilde{r}_{m,j} = \frac{\tilde{I}_j - I}{I} + \frac{D_I}{I} \qquad (22)$$

where I is the current level of the index and D_I is the point estimate dividend forecast for the index.

An assumption of linear monthly change has been made since a time path for price movements over the next twelve months was not specified nor, in light of the arguments presented earlier in this chapter, would it have been reasonable to try to collect such data. It is also assumed that 1/12 of the yearly dividend will be received each month. These assumptions are necessary for both the index and all equity securities to generate forecasts which have the same time horizon as the frequency of the feedback evaluation. Unless an assumption of this type were made, there is no clear way to incorporate the monthly information from new forecasts or the observed pattern of price behavior into revised forecasts during the year.

Given the linearity assumption, which at this point is needed to justify the inclusion of $12R_f$ and later to justify the division of estimated yearly return by 12, to obtain estimated monthly return:

$$\tilde{m}_j = \frac{\tilde{I}_j - I}{I} - 12R_f \qquad (23)$$

where $\tilde{m}_j$ is the conditional, excess, yearly market price return.

Dividend income is excluded from $\tilde{m}_j$ because in the context of the model dividends are not treated as random variables. The risk free rate, however, is included to facilitate an assumption needed later in the portfolio model of zero covariance between $\tilde{m}$ and $\tilde{m}^2$.

Since $\tilde{m}_j$ is a linear transformation of $\tilde{I}_j$, $\tilde{m}_j$ is also uniformly distributed, e.g.

$$f(\tilde{m}_j) = \begin{cases} \dfrac{1}{{}_H m_j - {}_L m_j} & {}_L m_j \leq \tilde{m}_j \leq {}_H m_j \\ 0 & \text{otherwise} \end{cases} \qquad (24)$$

where $_Lm_j = (_LI_j - I - 12R_f)/I$ and $_Hm_j = (_HI_j - I - 12R_f)/I$.

Prior to continuing the analysis of market price return it may be helpful to note that the rth moment of a uniform distribution of $_Ix$ is given by:

$$\mu_r = \frac{b^{r+1} - a^{r+1}}{(r+1)(b-a)}, \text{ where } a \leq \tilde{x} \leq b \qquad (25)$$

Freund [37] also contains a proof of the familiar relationship between the variance of a random variable and the moments of its distribution:

$$VAR(\tilde{x}) = \mu_2 - \mu_1^2 \qquad (26)$$

The expected value operator is applied to (23) to compute the conditional, expected, monthly, excess, price return:

$$\frac{E(\tilde{m}_j)}{12} = M_j = \frac{E(I_j) - I}{12I} - R_f$$

Using (25) with $r = 1$ and simplifying:

$$M_j = (_HI_j + {_LI_j} - 2I - 24IR_f)/24I \qquad (27)$$

or using (24)

$$M_j = (_Hm_j + {_Lm_j})/24 \qquad (28)$$

The unconditional, monthly, excess market price return employed in the portfolio algorithm can be found by computing:

$$M = \sum_{j=1}^{3} p_j M_j \qquad (29)$$

Computing the variance of $\tilde{m}_j$ is complicated by the fact that analysts were estimating uncertainty in their forecasts for twelve months, not one month ahead. The linear monthly change assumption made earlier can be translated into mathematical terms as:

$$\tilde{f}_t = a_1 + a_2 t + \tilde{e} \tag{30}$$

where f_t is the forecast for t months ahead, and a_1 and a_2 are constants for the current forecast.

Brown [28] has shown that if the forecaster is a squared error minimizer, uses (30) to form expectations, and adjusts his estimates of a_1 and a_2 by an exponential smoothing process, then the variance of the forecast can be estimated by:

$$\text{VAR}(\tilde{f}_t) = \alpha(1.25 + \alpha t)\sigma_e^2 \tag{31}$$

where α is the smoothing parameter, t is the forecast horizon and σ_e^2 is the underlying variance of the process.

Given (31) and Brown's assumptions which appear to be reasonable for the SDM data, the ratio of the variance of a one month forecast to the variance of a twelve month forecast is:

$$V = \text{VAR}(f_1)/\text{VAR}(f_{12}) = (1.25 + \alpha)/(1.25 + 12\alpha) \tag{32}$$

The value of α in turn is estimated by computing that α which would generate a smoothed series with the same average data age as a J period moving average. The value of α, therefore, is computed according to:

$$\alpha = \frac{2}{J + 1} \tag{33}$$

In the majority of the empirical tests conducted in Chapter 5, J is assigned a value of 12 months. Hence, an $\alpha = 2/13$ or .154 is used to be consistent

84 / A New Look at Portfolio Management

with the basic 12 month moving outlook of the analyst. The variance ratio V in this case is equal to .453.

Given the adjustment factor V, the conditional variance of $\tilde{m}_j$ translated from twelve months to one month can now be found by a direct application of (25), (26) and (32):

$$\sigma_{M_j}^2 = V\left(\left[\frac{_Hm_j^3 - {_L}m_j^3}{3(_Hm_j - {_L}m_j)}\right] - \left[\frac{_Hm_j^2 - {_L}m_j^2}{2(_Hm_j - {_L}m_j)}\right]^2\right)$$

This simplifies to:

$$\sigma_{M_j}^2 = V(_Hm_j - {_L}m_j)^2/12 \tag{34}$$

and the unconditional variance is:

$$\sigma_M^2 = \sum_{j=1}^{3} p\, \sigma_{M_j}^2 \tag{35}$$

Equations (24), (28), (29), (32), (34), and (35)—plus the knowledge that monthly dividend return in $D_I/12I$—are sufficient to compute the mean and variance of the monthly excess market return from the data generated through SDM.

In the traditional use of Beta models, β is assumed to be constant and independent of the level of R_m. Recent analysis of *ex post* data by Smidt and Brenner [70] as well as observations by the author of *a priori* SDM forecasts suggest that this assumption may be invalid. In a subsequent section, a non-linear Beta model is developed which does not make this independence assumption. At this point, therefore, it is useful to establish the properties of $\tilde{m}_j^2$, a variable used in the non-linear model. The approach is identical to that taken for $\tilde{m}_j$.

By using (25) with $r = 2$:

$$E(\tilde{m}_j/12)^2 = Q_j = \frac{_Hm_j^3 - {_L}m_j^3}{3(_Hm_j - {_L}m_j)(12)^2} \quad \text{or}$$

$$Q_j = \frac{_Hm_j^2 + {_H}m_{jL}m_j + {_L}m_j^2}{432} \tag{36}$$

The unconditional expected squared excess monthly market price return is then:

$$Q = \sum_{j=1}^{3} p_j Q_j \tag{37}$$

Again, by applying (25,) (26) and (32):

$$\sigma_{Q_j}^2 = V(4_H m_j^4 - {}_H m_j^3{}_L m_j - 6_H m_j^2{}_L m_j^3 + 4_L m_j^4)/45 \tag{38}$$

The unconditional variance is given by:

$$\sigma_Q^2 = \sum_{j=1}^{3} p_j \sigma_{Q_j} \tag{39}$$

This completes the development of the porperties of market return required by the portfolio management algorithm. The discussion now turns to an analysis of security returns.

SECURITY RETURNS

In Chapter 3 the triangular distribution format in which analysts submitted conditional price forecasts is introduced and illustrated by several numerical examples. In this section the properties of the conditional, triangular price distributions are examined, and algebraic expressions for price return and variance are developed.

For the jth market environment the price of a security is assumed to be triangularly distributed, e.g.

$$f(P_j) = \begin{cases} \dfrac{2}{({}_H P_j - {}_L P_j)} \left(\dfrac{\tilde{P}_j - {}_L \tilde{P}_j}{{}_M P_j - {}_L P_j} \right) & \text{if } {}_L P_j \leq \tilde{P}_j \leq {}_M P_j \\ \dfrac{2}{({}_H P_j - {}_L P_j)} \left(\dfrac{{}_H P_j - \tilde{P}_j}{{}_H P_j - {}_M P_j} \right) & \text{if } {}_M P_j \leq \tilde{P}_j \leq {}_H P_j \\ 0 & \text{otherwise} \end{cases} \tag{40}$$

where $_LP_j$ is the lowest price for the security in market j, $_MP_j$ is the most likely price, and $_HP_j$ is the highest price in market j.

The expected conditional price and its variance are by definition given by:

$$E(\tilde{P}_j) = \bar{P}_j = \int_{_LP_j}^{_HP_j} \tilde{P}_j f(\tilde{P}_j) dP_j \quad \text{and} \tag{41}$$

$$\sigma_{\tilde{P}_j}^2 = \int_{_LP_j}^{_HP_j} (\tilde{P}_j - \bar{P}_j)^2 f(\tilde{P}_j) dP_j \tag{42}$$

Solving equations (41) and (42) by integration by parts yields:

$$\bar{P}_j = (_HP_j + _MP_j + _LP_j)/3 \quad \text{and} \tag{43}$$

$$\sigma_{P_j}^2 = (_HP_j^2 + _MP_j^2 + _LP_j^2 - _HP_{jL}P_j - _HP_{jM}P_j - _MP_{jL}P_j)/18 \tag{44}$$

Equations (43) and (44), however, are in terms of price level and not excess price return. Conditional yearly excess price return is defined as:

$$\tilde{r}_j = \frac{\tilde{P}_j - P}{P} - 12R_f \tag{45}$$

where P is the current price of the security.

Taking expectations and dividing by 12 to adjust to monthly returns:

$$\frac{E(\tilde{r}_j)}{12} = R_j = \frac{E(\tilde{P}_j) - P}{12P} - R_f \quad \text{or}$$

$$R_j = (\bar{P}_j - P)/12P - R_f \tag{46}$$

The variance of R_j can be computed by noting that $VAR(\tilde{x}/a) =$

VAR(x̄)/a² and by recalling the forecast horizon factor V from (32). Therefore:

$$\sigma_{R_j}^2 = V\sigma_{P_j}^2/P^2 \tag{47}$$

The unconditional variance is obtained in the same manner as for market return, e.g.

$$\sigma_R^2 = \sum_{j=1}^{3} p_j \, \sigma_R^{2j} \tag{48}$$

Now that the statistical properties of security and market return forecasts are specified, the discussion turns to estimating the relationships between these forecasts.

SUBJECTIVE NON-LINEAR BETA MODEL

The two low cost portfolio management models in Table 4.1 are both beta model formulations. Beta models, however, are criticized in Chapter 2 for their instability. This critique is based on the observation that beta models estimated from past data appear to be poor estimates of current and future relationships. It is not a critique of their theoretical appropriateness. The strategy in this research is to take advantage of the computational advantages afforded by beta models, but to estimate them from *a priori* rather than *ex post* data. *A priori* rather than *ex post* estimation is also the theoretically valid approach. The criteria for evaluating the appropriateness of *a priori* beta models is their ability to convey current subjective beliefs as opposed to long term *ex post* stability of model coefficients.

Figure 4.1 highlights the method and assumptions involved in transforming security and market excess returns* generated by SDM into beta model representations. The assumptions made are:

---

* Recall that excess returns are returns minus the 30 day Treasury Bill return.

88 / *A New Look at Portfolio Management*

Figure 4.1

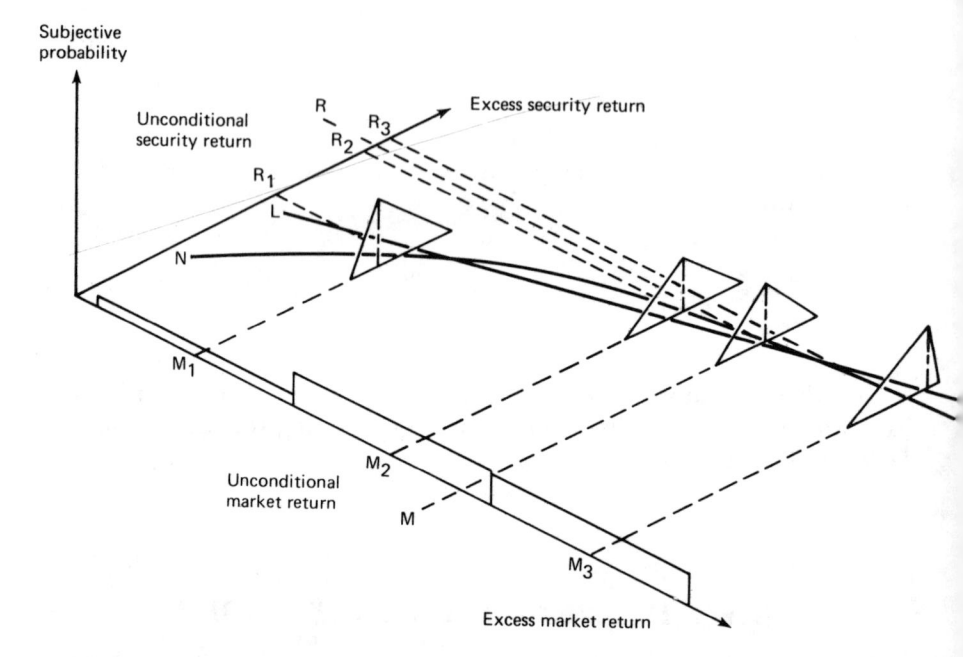

1. When analysts supply price estimates for a given market range, they implicitly form these estimates conditionally on the most likely point in this range. Since the market distributions are assumed to be uniform, this coincides with the expected market return in each possible environment.

2. Had analysts been asked to make forecasts conditional on other points within the market ranges, the means of these distributions would have fallen on the curve labeled NN in Figure 4.1. The assumption is also made, that curve NN can be estimated by fitting a quadratic function to the points (R_1,M_1), (R_2,M_2) and (R_3,M_3).

3. Although the subjective forecast variances may exhibit heteroscedasticity,* the simplifying assumption is made that forecast variance is homoscedastic. In the context of Figure 4.1, the variance of return is estimated from the three subjective distribution variances according to (48) and, in the portfolio management model, this variance is not a function of m.

The rationale behind these assumptions is that analysts would tend to shift their forecasts gradually in accordance with small changes in the forecasted, excess market return, rather than in large jumps. This same assumption underlies the linear beta model of capital market theory.

Figure 4.1 illustrates the operation of the estimated non-linear beta model. The shaded triangular distributions show conditional forecasts made by the analysts. The shaded uniform or rectangular distributions represent market returns forecasted by management and have been scaled to reflect different probabilities for the occurrence of each market environment. The unshaded distribution represents the unconditional return distribution calculated from the non-linear model, given the value of the unconditional excess market return from (29). The variance of this distribution is computed by (48) and, given assumption 3, is the same for all possible values of M. The use of mean and variance to characterize security distributions might at first appear to rule out any considerations of skewness. Although the inferred distribution is symmetric, its location is a function of the conditional skewness estimates. This approach has been taken as a compromise between the added complexity and question-

---

* For the nontechnical reader, heteroscedasticity refers to the combined effect of changes in the range of possible security returns and the most likely return as forecasts are based on different possible market returns.

able stability of explicit measures of skewness and the desire to incorporate estimates of significant skewness by analysts. Finally, the line LL illustrates a linear alternative to the non-linear model. Procedures for estimating LL are presented later in this section.

The monthly, non-linear, beta model is defined as:

$$\frac{\tilde{r}_j}{12} = \alpha + \beta \frac{\tilde{m}_j}{12} + \gamma \left(\frac{\tilde{m}_j}{12}\right)^2 + \tilde{\xi} \qquad (49)$$

Taking expectations, and assuming $E(\epsilon) = 0$:

$$R_j = \alpha + \beta M_j + \gamma Q_j \qquad (50)$$

Equations (28), (36) and (46) plus the SDM data can be used to generate R_j, M_j and Q_j. Given that we have an equation in three unknowns, α, β and γ, and three sets of observations, Cramer's Rule can be employed to solve for α, β and γ. Cramer's determinate equation for α is:

$$\alpha = \frac{\begin{vmatrix} R_1 & M1 & Q_1 \\ R_2 & M_2 & Q_1 \\ R_3 & M_3 & Q_3 \end{vmatrix}}{\begin{vmatrix} 1 & M_1 & Q_1 \\ 1 & M_2 & Q_2 \\ 1 & M_3 & Q_3 \end{vmatrix}}$$

Solving (51) yields:

$$\alpha = (R_1(M_2Q_3 - M_3Q_2) - R_2(M_1Q_3 - M_3Q_1) + R_3(M_1Q_2 - M_2Q_1))/D$$

where $D = (M_2Q_3 - M_3Q_2) - (M_1Q_3 - M_3Q_1) + (M_1Q_2 - M_2Q_1)$. (52)

Both β and γ be found in an identical fashion:

$$\beta = ((R_2Q_2 - R_3Q_2) - (R_1Q_3 - R_3Q_1) + (R_1Q_2 - R_2Q_1))/D \qquad (53)$$

and

$$\gamma = ((M_2R_3 - M_3R_2) - (M_1R_3 - M_3R_1) + (M_1R_2 - M_2R_1))/D \qquad (54)$$

Even though the non-linear model may appear to add an important new dimension, the assumptions required to estimate it or the inability of analysts to perceive non-linearities may make it an unnecessary complication. To enable a test of this hypothesis, linear beta models, e.g. $\gamma = 0$ in (50), are constructed. In this case the number of points exceeds the number of coefficients by one, and least squares regression instead of Cramer's Rule is utilized. A direct application of the standard Gauss-Markoff equations for least squares estimation gives:

$$\beta = \frac{3 \sum_{j=1}^{3} R_j M_j - (\sum_{j=1}^{3} R_j)(\sum_{j=1}^{3} M_j)}{3 \sum_{j=1}^{3} M_j^2 - (\sum_{j=1}^{3} M_j)^2} \quad \text{and} \qquad (55)$$

after computing β by (51):

$$\alpha = \sum_{j=1}^{3} R_j - \beta \sum_{j=1}^{3} M_j/3 \qquad (56)$$

Unconditional return for the ith security now can be computed by:

$$_iR = \alpha_i + \beta_i M + \gamma_i Q \qquad (57)$$

Equations (49) through (57) provide a way to translate SDM subjective price forecasts into beta models. By constructing beta models directly from analysts' forecasts rather than the usual method of using past security and market returns, the computational advantage of Sharpe's portfolio management approach can be gained. At the same time the usual disadvantage can be eliminated—of needing to assume that future security returns will be related to future market returns in exactly the same fashion as they have been in the past.

Equation (57), unlike Sharpe's beta model, also permits the analyst to reflect changes in the relationship between security and market returns for varying levels of market return. In the event that he does not foresee such changes, the last term in (57) becomes zero and the equation simplifies to Sharpe's original formulation (1).

Equation (57), while more general than Sharpe's model, does not include potentially valuable information about the analyst's historical ability to estimate this relationship. If, for example, he were always 10 percent too high, then this should be incorporated by reducing $_iR$ in (57) by 10 percent prior to making portfolio revisions. The steps necessary to make this feedback correction are treated in the next section.

FEEDBACK CORRECTION TO SUBJECTIVE FORECASTS

The approach taken is to construct optimal, adaptive, linear correction models for each security in the universe based on an analysis of analyst's forecasting performance. Prior to discussing the adaptive procedures developed in this study to estimate these models, a brief introduction to non-adaptive correction models is presented along lines similar to Theil [74].

If we let F_t represent the forecast, however generated, A_t the actual outcome and e_t the forecast error, then:

$$A_t = F_t + e_t \text{ or}$$

$$e_t = A_t - F_t \qquad (58)$$

Forecasts will be optimal if they are unbiased, i.e. $E(e) = 0$, and if they generate the least possible squared error, i.e. min $E(e^2)$.* In the following material, linearly corrected forecasts are formulated and shown to be optimal correctors in this context.

* E indicates expected or long run average value.

By squaring (58), taking expectations and collecting terms:

$$E(e^2) = \underset{1}{(\bar{F} - \bar{A})^2} + \underset{2}{(\sigma_F - r\sigma_A)^2} + \underset{3}{(1 - r^2)} \sigma_A^2 \qquad (59)$$

where r is the correlation between F and A and terms have been numbered for subsequent reference.

Linearly corrected forecasts are generated by first estimating with least squares regression the coefficients a and b in:

$$A_t = a + b\, S_t + v_t \qquad (60)$$

where S_t is the subjective forecast for A_t and v_t is an error term.

Forecasts are then constructed according to (61):

$$F_t = a + b\, S_t \qquad (61)$$

When (61) is used to estimate F_t, the following observations can be made:

1. $\bar{F} = a + \overline{bS}$ which in turn, by virtue of least squares estimation, equals $\bar{A}$. Term 1, therefore, equals 0 and, since it must always be positive or zero, 1 is also at its minimum value.

2. In (60), again by virtue of least squares:

$$b = \frac{r\, \sigma_A}{\sigma_S} \qquad (62)$$

where r is the correlation between A and S.

From the properties of standard deviation:

$$\sigma_F = \sigma_{(a + bS)} = b\, \sigma_S \tag{63}$$

Substituting (62) into (63) yields:

$$\sigma_F = r\, \sigma_A \tag{64}$$

Substitution of (64) into (59) shows that erms 2 is also equal to 0 and is at its minimum value.

3. Since (61) is a linear transformation and r in (59) is invariant under linear transformations, term 3 is not effected by the values of a and b in (61).

Consequently, given the underlying process generating S_t, linear correction of S_t as defined by (60) and (61) will minimize the value of $E(e^2)$. The corrected forecasts will also be unbiased since:

$$E(v) = 0$$

due to least squares estimation of (60) and the observation that:

$$v_t = A_t - F_t = e_t$$

The optimality of the forecast is a limited optimality, however, as it assumes a and b to be constants and does not consider ways to increase the value of r. In SDM, the return reports and management review of feedback measures were designed to improve r. Any benefits in terms of increased r, therefore, are already contained in the SDM data. On the other hand, adaptive estimates of a and b can be computed and should help to reduce error variances due to any instability in these coefficients.

The first step in estimating adaptive a and b requires a redefinition of the criteria for optimal correction. Unbiasedness in terms of $E(e) = 0$ is retained, but the squared error criteria in (60) is altered to put greater weight on more recent errors and to reflect a growing history of past errors. In algebraic terms:

$$\min E\left(\sum_{t=-T}^{0} v_t^2 (-\alpha)^{-t} \right) \tag{65}$$

A General Pension Fund Management Simulator / 95

where T is the number of periods of past observations and α is between 0 and 1 and indicates the rate of discount of past errors.

Substituting $A_t - a - b\ S_t$ from (60) for v_t in (65), differentiating (65) with respect to a and b and setting each equation equal to 0 in order to solve for a minimum, yields the following equation system:

$$\begin{pmatrix} \sum_{t=-T}^{0} (1-\alpha)^{-t} & \sum_{t=-T}^{0} S_t(1-\alpha)^{-t} \\ \sum_{t=-T}^{0} S_t(1-\alpha)^{-t} & \sum_{t=-T}^{0} S_t^2(1-\alpha)^{-t} \end{pmatrix} \begin{pmatrix} a \\ b \end{pmatrix} = \begin{pmatrix} \sum_{t=-T}^{0} A_t(1=\alpha)^{-t} \\ \sum_{t=-T}^{0} A_t S_t(1-\alpha)^{-t} \end{pmatrix} \quad (66)$$

Letting $\delta_t = (1 - \alpha)^{-t}$ and noting that all sums run from $-T$ to 0, (66) can be solved by premultiplying both sides of (66) by the inverse of the forecast data matrix to give:

$$\begin{pmatrix} a \\ b \end{pmatrix} = \frac{\begin{pmatrix} \Sigma\ S_t^2 \delta_t & -\Sigma\ S_t \delta_t \\ -\Sigma\ S_t \delta_t & \Sigma \delta_t \end{pmatrix} \begin{pmatrix} \Sigma A_t S_t \\ \Sigma A_t S_t \delta_t \end{pmatrix}}{(\Sigma\ \delta_t)\ (\Sigma\ S_t^2 \delta_t) - (\Sigma\ S_t \delta_t)^2} \quad (67)$$

Equation (67) can be estimated for large T or small α by first observing that:

$$\lim_{T \to \infty} \delta_t = \lim_{T \to \infty} \sum_{t=-T}^{0} (1 - \alpha)^{-t} - \alpha^{-1} \quad (68)$$

and that for any variable $_jX_T$ defined by:

$$_jX_T = \sum_{t=-T}^{0} {_jx_t}(1 - \alpha)^{-t}$$

it follows that:

$$_jX_{T+1} = {_jx_0} + (1 - \alpha)_j X_T \quad (69)$$

96 / A New Look at Portfolio Management

Transforming the subscripts of X to indicate time relative to the current period, (69) becomes:

$$_jX_0 = {}_jx_0 + (1 - \alpha)_jX_{-1} \tag{70}$$

Rewriting (67) using (68) and (70):

$$\begin{pmatrix} a \\ b \end{pmatrix} = \frac{\begin{pmatrix} {}_1X_0 & -{}_2X_0 \\ -{}_2X_0 & \alpha^{-1} \end{pmatrix} \begin{pmatrix} {}_3X_0 \\ {}_4X_0 \end{pmatrix}}{(\alpha^{-1})_1X_0 - ({}_2X_0)^2} \tag{71}$$

The adaptive formulas for the $_jX_0$ are simple equations in terms of the last value computed, e.g. $_jX_{-1}$, the forecast made last period and the current period actual. When the subjective forecast $_iR$ from (57) is substituted for S and A represents the actual excess monthly price return, these equations become:

$$_1X_0 = {}_1R_0^2 + (1 - \alpha)_1X_{-1} \tag{72}$$

$$_2X_0 = {}_1R_0 + (1 - \alpha)_2X_{-1} \tag{73}$$

$$_3X_0 = {}_1A_0 + (1 - \alpha)_3X_{-1} \quad \text{and} \tag{74}$$

$$_4X_0 = {}_1A_{0i}R_0 + (1 - \alpha)_4X_{-1} \tag{75}$$

Initialization values are 0 for all $_jX_{-1}$ when T = 0.

Thus equations (71) through (75) plus (33) to compute α can be used to optimally, and adaptively correct the next forecast, S_1, based on the discounted experience of prior forecasting errors.

Feedback correction for M and Q follows directly from (61):

$$M^c = a_M + b_M M \quad \text{and} \tag{76}$$

$$Q^c = a_Q + b_Q Q$$

Equation (57) may now be expanded to include feedback information in the non-linear beta model. Using (61), for each security:

$$_iR^c = a_i + b_i \,_iR \tag{77}$$

where $_iR^c$ is the corrected forecast.
Substituting (57) for $_iR$ and using (77):

$$_iR^c = a_i + b_i(\alpha_i + \beta_i M^c + \gamma_i Q^c) \text{ which simplifies to}$$

$$_iR^c = (a + b\alpha)_i + (b\beta)_i M^c + (b\gamma)^i Q^c \tag{78}$$

If there is no bias, e.g. all $a_i = 0$ and $b_i = 1$, then (78) reduces to (57).

The discussion of feedback correction has, so far, been limited to modification of the level of return. Level modifications also alter the variance of return. Equation (48), when feedback correction in the form of (61) takes place for the i security, becomes:

$$_i\sigma_R^2 = b_i^2 \,_i\sigma_R^{2c} \tag{79}$$

Equation (79), however, does not utilize feedback on the analyst's assessment of uncertainty. The inclusion of b_i^2 only adjusts the analyst's variance to be consistent with the corrected level of return. It is important

98 / A New Look at Portfolio Management

to recall that the analyst is forecasting uncertainty relative to a market level. Consequently, the analyst's effective error q_t is defined by:

$$q_t = A_t - (R_t^c | \text{actual market return in t}) \tag{80}$$

A least squares estimate of the actual error variance can be made by smoothing the first and second moments of q_t, e.g.

$$_tq_1 = \alpha\, q_t + (1 - \alpha)_{t-1}q_1 \quad \text{and} \tag{81}$$

$$_tq_2 = \alpha\, q_t^2 + (1 - \alpha)_{t-1}q_2 \tag{82}$$

where $_tq_j$ is the j moment of q_t estimated as of t.
Recalling (26):

$$\text{Var}(\tilde{x}) = \mu_2 - \mu_1^2$$

The smoothed estimate at time t can be estimated by:

$$\text{Var}_t(\tilde{q}) \approx {_tq_2} - {_tq_1^2} \tag{83}$$

A variance correction factor can now be estimated for each forecast supplied through SDM by combining (79), (83) and (49):

$$_iC_t = \alpha\, \text{Var}_t(\tilde{q})/_i\sigma_R^{2c} + (1 - \alpha)\, _iC_{t-1} \tag{84}$$

where $_iC_t$ is the variance correction factor and $_i\sigma_R^{2c}$ was estimated in $t - 1$ for t using (79) and (49).

The variance included in the portfolio algorithm for each security when both level and variance feedback takes place is found by:

$$s_I^2 = {}_IC_t \, {}_I\sigma_R^{2c} \tag{85}$$

where ${}_I\sigma_R^{2c}$ is the estimate for t + 1, and s_I^2 represents the current expected variance in price return for the next month, taking all available subjective forecasts and feedback evaluation into account.

Again, the same steps are repeated to correct for level and variance feedback for M and Q. Hence:

$$s_M^2 = {}_MC_t \, b_M^2 \, \sigma_M^2 \text{ where } \sigma_M^2 \text{ is computed by (35) and} \tag{86}$$

$$s_Q^2 = {}_QC_t \, b_Q^2 \sigma_Q^2 \text{ where } \sigma_Q^2 \text{ is computed by (39).} \tag{87}$$

The tools necessary to transform conditional price forecasts made by security analysts into subjective Beta models which include market level and feedback effects are now in hand. The analysis turns in the next section to using these tools to construct models of the pension fund management problem.

OBJECTIVE FUNCTION: VARIANCE

In this section the pension fund management problem is developed along lines similar to Sharpe's diagonal model. The variance of the portfolio is estimated, as it is in the diagonal model, in terms of the variance of the market and the coefficients and variance of security Beta models. Later sections treat alternative objective functions, such as responsiveness, which may be equally effective and, as indicated in Table 4.1, much less expensive to implement.

The components of return are much more extensive and detailed, however, than those used by Sharpe. In general terms:

$$\begin{aligned}
\text{Pension Fund Return} = &\sum_{\text{securities}} \text{Capital appreciation} \quad (88)\\
&+ \sum_{\text{securities}} \text{,dividends}\\
&+ \text{Captial appreciation of market fund}\\
&+ \text{Dividend return from market fund}\\
&+ \text{Short term bond return}\\
&- \sum_{\text{securities}} \text{Trading and transaction costs}\\
&- \text{Trading and transaction costs for market fund}\\
&- \text{Transaction costs for bonds}\\
&- \sum_{\text{securities}} \text{Management fees}\\
&- \text{Management fees for market fund}\\
&- \text{Management fees for bonds}
\end{aligned}$$

Portfolio return, defined by (88), takes into account that pension fund managers consider trade-offs such as:

1. Uncertain capital appreciation vs relatively certain dividend return.

2. Picking winners and incurring high trading and transaction costs vs investing in a Wells Fargo type of market fund with much lower costs and management fees.

3. Holding short-term bonds and reducing or completely withdrawing funds from the equity markets. Long-term bonds could have been included in the tests by translating yield curve forecasts into bond prices and building the corresponding beta models. Unfortunately, long-term interest rates were not forecasted in any formal fashion and, therefore, could not have been collected through SDM.

4. The benefits of lower return variability through selection of short-term bonds or the market portfolio were offset by reduced management fees.

Prior to translating (88) into algebraic terms, several variables which have not been discussed need to be introduced.

Management Fees

Management fees in pension fund management are stated in return dimensions as a percentage of asset value. In the following equations these fees will be represented by f_i for the ith asset managed. In practice the f_i's are usually the same for all assets in a given fund and for all funds of similar size managed by a single institution. In this research the effect of non-uniform fees is examined. For example, the management fee for the market fund is lower than the general equity security fee. The fee for managing the short-term bond portfolio is nominal and even lower than the market fund fee. The varying fees, of course, reflect alternative marketing approaches to pension fund management.

Flow Representation

The portfolio return can be expressed as a function of N individual asset returns, e.g.

$$\text{portfolio return} = \sum_{i=1}^{N} w_i (\text{asset return})_i \text{ and} \qquad (89)$$

$$\sum_{i=1}^{N} w_i = 1$$

Equation (89) is in terms of stock levels and not revision flows. The w_i's may be stated in terms of current holdings, h_i, and revision flows, z_i, as:

$$w_i = h_i + z_i \qquad (90)$$

where $\sum_{i=1}^{N} h_i = 1$ and

$$\sum_{i=1}^{N} z_i = 0$$

102 / *A New Look at Portfolio Management*

Equation (89) can now be expressed in current stock levels and revision flows as:

$$\text{portfolio return } \sum_{i=1}^{N} h_i(\text{asset return})_i + \sum_{i=1}^{N} z_i(\text{asset return})_i \quad (91)$$

Transaction Costs

Transaction costs greatly complicate the design of a portfolio management model from both a mathematical and theoretical viewpoint. The mathematical complication arises from the observation that transaction costs reduce return for both negative and positive revision flows. This requires the use of an absolute value formulation:

$$\text{Transaction cost} = \sum_{i=1}^{N} t_i |z_i| \quad (92)$$

where t_i is the transaction cost in percentage units and may be dependent upon the magnitude, sign and timing of z_i within the revision period.

The transaction cost for each asset is composed of brokerage commissions plus liquidity costs on sales or price increases on buys due to market thinness. Although the brokerage costs are known and, for the volume traded by institutions, a fixed percentage, the market costs have been estimated by traders in the participating institutions to be anywhere between 0 percent for a passive strategy to as much as 10 percent for an active program. Given the active trading style of the institution which provided the SDM data and its reluctance to incur excess trading costs—achieved by putting limits on $|z_i|$, t_i is assumed to be greater than zero, constant and independent of z_i. This assumption could easily be relaxed by using the piecewise approximation procedure suggested by Pogue [58]. However, in light of the increased solution costs and very subjective nature of the market effect forecasts, this further complication does not seem warranted.

Expected Return

Equation (88) for unconditional, expected portfolio return can now be written in the following algebraic form:

$$R_p = \sum_{i=1}^{N-2} w_i({}_1R^c + R_f) \quad \text{(equity appreciation)} \quad (93)$$

$$+\sum_{i=1}^{N-2} w_i(_iD/_iP) \quad \text{(equity dividends)}$$

$$+w_{N-1}(M^c + R_f) \quad \text{(market fund appreciation)}$$

$$+w_{N-1}\,_1D/I \quad \text{(market dividend)}$$

$$+w_N R_f \quad \text{(short-term bond)}$$

$$-\sum_{i=1}^{N-2} t_i|z_i| \quad \text{(equity transaction costs)}$$

$$-|t_{N-1}\,z_{N-1}| \quad \text{(market fund trans. costs)}$$

$$-t_N\,z_N \quad \text{(bond purchase costs, short-term bonds cannot be sold prior to maturity)}$$

$$-\sum_{i=1}^{N-2} w_i\,f_i \quad \text{(equity management fees)}$$

$$-w_{N-1}f_{N-1} \quad \text{(market fund fee)}$$

$$-w_N\,f_N \quad \text{(bond fee)}$$

Equation (93) can be simplified if in (78), which defines the components of $_iR^c$, we let $\alpha_{N-1} = 0$, $\beta_{N-1} = 1$ and $\gamma_{N-1} = 0$ for the market fund, e.g. i = N−1 and $_NR^c = {}_ND = 0$ for short-term bonds. This simply states that the market fund is the same as the index and that there are no equity components to short-term bond returns. Equation (93) can now be written as:

$$R_p = \sum_{i=1}^{N} w_i(_iR^c + {}_iD/_iP + R_f - f_i) - \sum_{i=1}^{N} t_i|z_i| \tag{94}$$

or expanding $_iR^c$ from (78).

$$R_p = \sum_{i=1}^{N} w_i((a + b\alpha)_i + {}_iD/_iP + R_f - f_i) + \sum_{i=1}^{N} w_i(b\beta)_i M^c + \sum_{i=1}^{N} w_i(b\gamma)_i Q^c + \sum_{i=1}^{N} w_i\,E_i(v) - \sum_{i=1}^{N} t_i|z_i| \tag{95}$$

where $E_i(v)$ is the expected value of the error in the corrected forecast and by construction equals 0 for all i.

Variance of Return

The variance of portfolio return can be computed from (95) by first noting that, in general:

$$\text{Var}(\sum_{i=1}^{N} a_i \tilde{x}_i) = \sum_{i=1}^{N} a_i^2 \text{Var}(\tilde{x}_i) + 2\sum_{i<j}^{N} a_i a_j \text{Cov}(\tilde{x}_i, \tilde{x}_j) \tag{96}$$

and secondly that:

$$\text{Var}(\text{constant}) = \text{Cov}(\text{constant}, \tilde{x}) = 0 \tag{97}$$

The first and last terms in (95) are not random variables and, therefore, have zero variance and covariances with all other terms. The variances of the second, third and fourth terms have already been analyzed and can be computed by (86), (87) and (85) respectively. In order to use (96), however, the covariances of these terms as well as their variances must be known. The covariance of v with M^c or Q^c is zero by virtue of the homogeneity assumptions and the least squares properties of (61).

The remaining $\text{Cov}(\tilde{M}^c, \tilde{Q}^c)$ is not equal to zero by assumption or construction, but because of empirical reasons it will be small and close to zero. This can be demonstrated by first considering the correlation between $\tilde{M}^c$ and $\tilde{Q}^c$. $\tilde{Q}^c$ is a quadratic function of $\tilde{M}^c$. This function is shown in Figure 4.2. If the expected excess market return is significantly positive or negative then $\tilde{Q}^c$ will be positively or negatively correlated with $\tilde{M}^c$. If, however, the expected value of $\tilde{M}^c$ is near zero, then, given the uniform distribution assumption for $\tilde{M}^c$, both the correlation and the covariance between $\tilde{M}^c$ and $\tilde{Q}^c$ will be near zero. This is an excellent example of the case when even though two variables are causally related they may still not be correlated. The use of excess return instead of market return improves this approximation. The mean of the actual excess monthly return over the period examined is $-.0013$. Hence, the $\text{Cov}(\tilde{M}^c, \tilde{Q}^c)$ is estimated to be sufficiently close to zero, to use zero for its value.

A General Pension Fund Management Simulator / **105**

Figure 4.2.

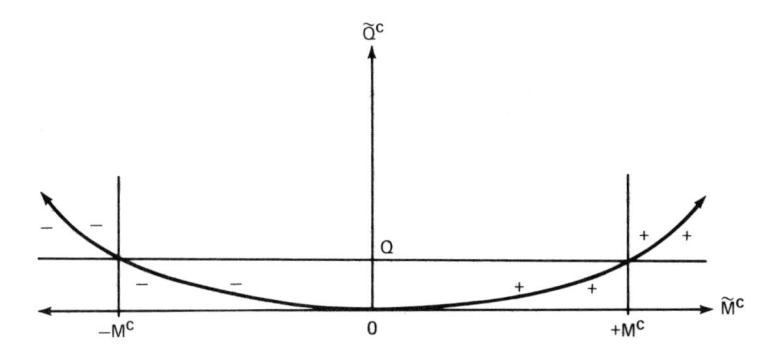

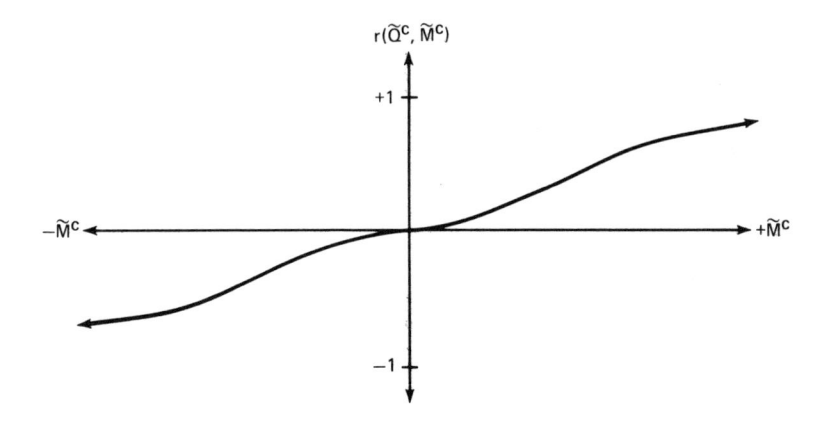

106 / *A New Look at Portfolio Management*

The feedback corrected variance of portfolio return, therefore, is given by:

$$s_p^2 = \sum_{i=1}^{N-1} w_i(b\beta)_i)^2 s_M^2 + (\sum_{i=1}^{N-1} w_i(b\gamma)_i)^2 s_Q^2 + \sum_{i=1}^{N-1} w_i^2 s_i^2 \qquad (98)$$

The sums in (98) need only go up to $N-1$ since the Nth asset is the zero variance riskless bond.

Objective Function

The objective function may now be stated in the standard mean variance form using (94) and (98) as:

$$\max R_p - K_1 s_p^2 \qquad (99)$$

where K_1 is a risk-return trade-off parameter.

When upper bounds, u_i, on the w_i are employed, as they must be in pension fund management to satisfy Prudent Man diversification norms, Stone [73] has suggested an approximation which makes (99) linear in w_i. Stone proposed a substitution of $u_i w_i$ for w_i^2 in the third term of s_p^2. When $w_i = 0$ or $w_i = u_i$ there is no error. In fact, due to the quadratic programming properties of (99) at most one w_i will not be equal to zero or u_i. For minimal Prudent Man requirements of 20 or more securities, this error should be negligible. Given this approximation and a similar approximation which assumes any security in the approved universe is equally likely to be selected, s_p^2 can be estimated very well by:

$$s_p^2 \approx (\sum_{i=1}^{N-1} w_i(b\beta)_i) (\sum_{i=1}^{N-1} u_i(b\beta)_i) s_M^2 / \sum_{i=1}^{N} u_i \qquad (100)$$

$$+ (\sum_{i=1}^{N-1} w_i(b\gamma)_i) (\sum_{i=1}^{N-1} u_i(b\gamma)_i) s_Q^2 / \sum_{i=1}^{N} u_i$$

$$+ \sum_{i=1}^{N-1} w_i u_i s_i^2$$

The first two terms in (100) must be divided by $\sum_{i=1}^{N} u_i$ to include the constraint that:

$$\sum u_j = 1$$
j∈{securities held out of N approved}

Although (99) using (100) to estimate s_p^{2*} may be solved at low cost, the variance approach to risk measurement was demonstrated in Chapter 3 to be inappropriate for pension fund management. Table 4.1 indicates that Baumol's measure of risk is appropriate. Baumol maximizes the lowest value a portfolio might return subject to a small probability of doing even worse. This safety-first orientation is very consistent with current Prudent Man requirements. In Figure 4.3 risk is expressed by the probability that return will indeed fall below a minimum level $R_p - K s_p$. The objective is to maximize this level of return given the risk probability. This diagram corresponds closely with the description of pension fund risks in Figure 3.10. The distribution of portfolio returns is pictured as a normal distribution in Figure 4.3. Unpublished studies conducted by the institution in which SDM was installed confirmed the power of the central limit theorem. Return distributions were not significantly different from normal even when as few as fifteen securities were included in the portfolio. This finding permits a direct translation of any risk probability p by the use of standard tables for the normal distribution into a value for K_1. Unfortunately (99) and (100) are functions of s_p^2 not s_p. If, however, in (99) K_1 were established so that:

$$K_1 = K/\hat{s}_p \tag{101}$$

and K were computed as a function of the risk probability p and $\hat{s}_p$ were an estimate of the portfolio variance, then maximizing (99) would be equivilent to a safety first approach to risk. Fortunately, as discussed below, it is feasible to estimate $\hat{s}_p$ and to incorporate this approximation into Sharpe-Stone-Baumol framework.

*For the managerially oriented reader, s_p^2 measures the combined effect on the uncertainty of portfolio return of the security analysts' current uncertainties and past forecasting errors for all securities included in the portfolio.

108 / *A New Look at Portfolio Management*

Figure 4.3

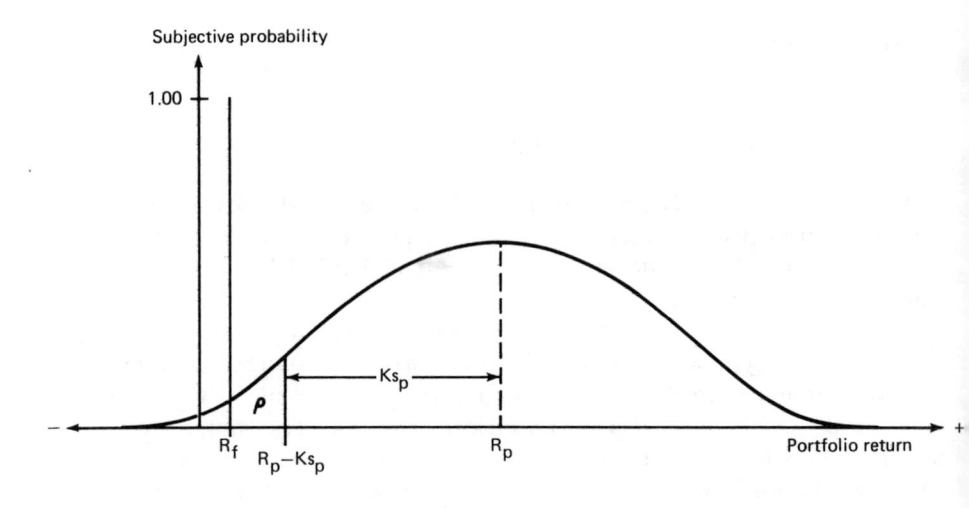

Sharpe observed that the contribution of the third term in s_p^2, nonsystematic risk, declines linearly with further diversification while the contributions of systematic risk, represented by the first two terms in s_p^2 are not effected by diversification.* Sharpe [60] also made the reasonable assumption that the average non-systematic risk is approximately equal to the average systematic risk for a well-diversified portfolio. If $\bar{u}_i$ represents the average upper bound, then, given Sharpe's assumptions:

$$\text{portfolio variance} \approx (\text{Systematic risk})/(1 - \bar{u}_i)$$

The second term in (100) will also tend to be a factor of 10 or more smaller than the first term. The values of M historically average out to less than .01, explaining why $s_Q^2 \ll s_M^2$. Even though skewness, as captured by γ, may be important in selecting individual securities, the tendency toward normality for the portfolio as a whole combined with the linear approximation for w_i^2 will cause the sum of the coefficients of s_Q^2 to approach 0. Thus, taking advantage of Stone's approximation and Sharpe's observations, the standard deviation of the portfolio can be estimated by:

$$\hat{s}_p \approx s_M (\sum_{i=1}^{N-1} u_i (b\beta)_i) / ((\sum_{i=1}^{N} u_i) (1 = \sum_{i=1}^{N} u_i/N)) \qquad (102)$$

As a conceptual check of (102), if $(b\beta)_i$ is symmetrically distributed about a mean of 1 and $u_i = 1/n$, where n is the number of securities required for diversification, then (102) would be approximately equal to $s_M(N/(n-1))$ or simply s_M for large n. The linearized, safety-first form of the objective function can now be written as:

$$\max R_P - (K/\hat{s}_p) s_p^2 \text{ or}$$

$$\max \sum_{i=1}^{N} w_i (_i R^c + {}_i D/{}_i P + R_f - f_i - K((b\beta)_i K_M + (b\gamma)_i K_Q$$

$$+ K_s u_i s_i^2) - \sum_{i=1}^{N} t_i |z_i| \qquad (103)$$

* Although this is true in theory because β and γ are assumed to be known with perfect certainty, in actuality diversification will also reduce the systematic risk by reducing the sampling variances of β_p and γ_p.

110 / *A New Look at Portfolio Management*

$$\text{where } K_M = s_M \left(1 - \sum_{i=1}^{N} u_i/N\right)$$

$$K_Q = \frac{\left(\sum_{i=1}^{N} u_i(b\gamma)_i\right)s_Q^2 \left(1 - \left(\sum_{i=1}^{N} u_i\right)/N\right)}{\left(\sum_{i=1}^{N} u_i(bB)_i\right)s_M}$$

$$K_s = 1/s_p$$

Furthermore, the coefficient of w_i in (103) is no longer a function of decision variables and may be represented by a constant, K_i^y, for the ith security. Rewriting (103):

$$\max \sum_{i=1}^{N} (w_i K_i^y - t|z_i|) \tag{104}$$

Even though (104) is much more tractable than (99), (104) still constains a mixture of stock level variables, the w_i's, and flow variables, the z_i's. Using the definition of w_i given by (90), (104) can be written as:

$$\max \sum_{i=1}^{N} ((h_i + z_i)K_i^y - t_i|z_i|) \text{ or}$$

$$\max \sum_{i=1}^{N} (z_i K_i^y - t_i|z_i|) + \max \sum_{i=1}^{N} h_i K_i^y \tag{105}$$

The last term in (105), however, is a constant and need not be considered in solving (105) for the revision flow variables. This last simplification reduces the variance-based, safety-first objective function discussed in this section to:

$$\max \sum_{i=1}^{N} (z_i K_i^y - t_i|z_i|) \tag{106}$$

$$\text{subject to: } \sum_{i=1}^{N} z_i = 0$$

In the absence of transaction costs and, therefore, the absolute value function in (106), (104) can be solved by simple ranking methods at very low cost. With inclusion of transaction costs, (106) is structurally a knapsack, dynamic programming problem. Fortunately, the upper bound constraints required to force Prudent Man diversification facilitate the development in the next section of a low cost, heuristic solution to (106) with transaction costs included.

In this section, the portfolio management problem has been reduced to computing for each security a numerical value, K_i^y, which incorporates portfolio risk and return goals, security forecasts, market forecasts and forecast feedback evaluations, then estimating transaction costs, t_i, for each security and finally solving (106) for the decision variables, z_i, i.e. $z_i < 0$ is a buy, $z_i > 0$ is a sell, and $z_i = 0$ is a hold. The risk and return goals assumed in computing K_i^y are consistent with the safety-first philosophy of Prudent Man investment norms. In the next section, a low cost method is developed to solve the portfolio revision problem expressed in (106).

REVISION ALGORITHM

The revision algorithm is primarily a ranking procedure which also does share and cash accounting. In order to make a description of this algorithm as clear and as concise as possible, its central features are first treated separately, then an overall summary flow chart is presented. This approach is taken in lieu of a detailed line by line development of the entire computer module which would cover mainly accounting and computer programming considerations.

Separate Buy and Sell Rankings

Intuitively, it might appear that the algorithm could be constructed around a single high to low ranking of $K_i - t_i$ with buys selected from the top of the list and sells starting with the bottom.* This would be a valid assumption only if transaction costs were identical for all securities. Table 4.2 illustrates the discrepancy between the actual sell rankings and the inverse of the buy rankings when, as in this study and in practice, transaction costs differ.

* Recall that the objective of the algorithm is to maximize the value of (106) and that $z_i > 0$ indicates a buy.

Table 4.2.

i	K_i	t_i	Buy	Rank	Sell	Rank	Buy Inverse
1	.02	.005	.015	1	−.025	5	7
2	.03	.02	.01	2	−.05	7	6
3	.01	.02	−.01	3	−.03	6	5
4	.00	.02	−.02	4	−.02	4	4
5	−.01	.02	−.03	5	−.01	3	3
6	−.02	.02	−.04	6	.00	2	2
7	−.03	.02	−.05	7	.01	1	1

Consequently, the revision algorithm first forms a buy ranking and then a sell ranking. The effort to do this, however, is not twice that required for a single ranking, since the inverse of the buy ranking is used as a starting point in determining the sell ranking. In the current version of this algorithm straight forward FORTRAN sorting methods are employed. In operational use a several fold improvement could be achieved by converting the algorithm to more efficient but more complex binary sort methods.

Flow Limits

The magnitude of the z_i's is limited by:

$$-h_i < z_i < u_i - h_i$$

The upper bound for R_f is set equal to 1 to permit a complete shift out of the equity markets into the risk free asset if the forecast warrant it, e.g. i = N for 30 day Treasury Bills or:

$$u_N = 1$$

The value of $K_N^y - t_N$ for the riskless asset is always positive.
The core of the algorithm contains the following steps:

1. Rank $K_i^y - t_i$ for buys.
2. Rank $K_i^y - t_i$ for sells.
3. Invest all available cash in the highest ranked buy unless z_i reaches its upper bound. In this event continue the process with the next highest buy.
4. When all available cash is exhausted in step 3, start selling with the highest ranked sell until z_i reaches its lower bound, provided that the marginal gain from investing in the best available buy is positive.
5. Given the data in Table 4.2, if we assume that security 1 is at the upper bound for z_1, then 7, and 6 if necessary, but no other securities would be sold to purchase 2.

The ability to invest in a risk free asset, which will always provide positive return, without an upper bound, means that no idle cash will be left and that all securities in the category of 6 and 7 in Table 4.2 will be liquidated.

Transaction Costs

Transaction costs complicate the algorithm well beyond the points already mentioned. In order to determine in step 3, for example, the number of shares which can be purchased of the first security on the buy list, the total value of the portfolio after revision must be known. By definition:

$$u_i = \frac{_iP\, L_i}{A - T_a}$$

where L_i is the number of shares,
A is the initial cash value of the portfolio and
T_a is the actual sum of transaction costs for revision

Or $\quad L_i = u_i(A - T_a) / {}_iP$ \hfill (107)

Unfortunately; T_a is not known until the last trade has been made. Although this type of problem can be solved by dynamic programming or by linear programming with separate buy and sell flow variables, the costs would be many times greater than for a ranking algorithm. The method, employed in the revision algorithm uses an estimate, T_e, for T_a and, if necessary, adjustment procedures should $|T_e - T_a|$ be greater than a specified tolerance level. If we let L_i^e indicate the value of (107) when T_e is used to estimate T_a, then:

$$L_i/L_i^e = (A - T_a) / (A - T_e) \text{ or as a correction to } L_i^e$$

$$\Delta L_i^e = \left[\frac{(A - T_a)}{(A - T_e)} - 1\right] L_i^e \text{ and} \hfill (108)$$

$$L_i = L_i^e + \Delta L_i^e$$

As shares of each security are adjusted to meet the u_i constraints, the actual transaction cost must also be corrected. This correction, however, should not double count transaction costs. Table 4.3 summarizes the

Table 4.3. Adjustments to T_a

		Initial Decision	
		Buy	Sell
Correction Adjustment	Buy	$+t_{i\ i}P\ \Delta L_i^e$	$-t_{i\ i}P\ \Delta L_i^e$
	Sell	$-t_{i\ i}P\ \Delta L_i^e$	$+t_{i\ i}P\ \Delta L_i^e$

adjustment logic to avoid such double counting during the correction phase.

Another complication introduced by transaction costs involves distinguishing between nominal and effective transaction costs. If, for example, in Table 4.2 security 1 is purchased and held for a year, and if the monthly return of .02 were to continue for the remainder of the year, then the annual rate of return would be .02(12) − .005, or .235. If the security were held for only 2 months, then the annualized return would be only 6(.02(2) − .005), or .21. The difference is due to the one time nature of the transaction cost and the limited one period return focus of the revision algorithm. All transaction costs, therefore, except the cost for purchasing one period risk free bonds, are converted to effective costs by scaling the nominal costs by an estimated, average holding period. If, for example, the average holding period were 4 months, then the effective transaction cost used in ranking the forecasted returns would be .005/(12/4), or .00125. Cash flows, however, would be computed using .005.

Final Adjustments

If some excess cash or deficit exists after the transaction cost corrections, the next available buy or sell is executed to drive the cash balance to zero. As the last step in the algorithm, the actual holdings or w_i for all securities are computed. Although these w_i will be much closer to either u_i or 0, with the exception of the w_i for the last security acted upon, than the initial w_i's arrived at using T_e, there could still be excessive variation. In this event the adjustment process would need to be repeated. After hundreds of runs of this revision algorithm, the single execution of the transaction cost adjustment has always yielded the solution to (106) within the significant digit capacity of the digital computer. A summary flow chart of the revision algorithm can be found at the end of this chapter.

OBJECTIVE FUNCTION: BETA

The development of pension fund management models has thus far been an extension of Sharpe's diagonal model simplification of Markowtiz's original work. Sharpe also observed that an even simpler approximation might work just as well and at less cost. He suggested that since the nonsystematic component of portfolio variance approached zero as diversification increased, this term could be dropped for large portfolios. In Sharpe's terminology:

$$\text{portfolio variance} \approx \beta_p^2 \text{ (market variance)} \qquad (109)$$

where $\beta_p = \sum_{i=1}^{N} w_i \beta_{s,i}$ and

$\beta_{s,i}$ is Sharpe's linear β, e.g., see (1).

He further proposed that decisions generated from just $\beta_{s,i}$, ignoring market variance, would do little to degrade the quality of the approximation. In a test of this hypothesis, Sharpe [63], found that 30 portfolios selected by $\beta_{s,i}$ criteria from a universe of 63 securities changed composition less than 3 percent when compared to the full Markowtiz algorithm solutions. In addition, Table 4.2 indicates that the simplicity of Sharpe's β formulation places it in the category of acceptable operating costs. There is, however, another major reason beyond cost effectiveness to develop a Beta model formulation of the objective function. In Chapter 2 the three principal forms of risk adjusted performance measures are given in equations (3), (4) and (5). If a fund manager were measured by Sharpe's reward to variability, (4), then it would be consistent for him to use the objective function based on variance, (106). On the other hand, if he were evaluated by Treynor's reward to volatility (3) or Jensen's differential return (5), then a β formulated objective function would be theoretically more appropriate. One of the hypotheses tested in Chapter 5 questions whether in practice selection of different performance measures has any significant impact on portfolio composition or performance. In this section, therefore, a β formulated objective function is developed. This formulation is more complex than Sharpe's due to a combination of the non-linear return model, transaction costs and the necessity to control the downside risk to permit comparison between full variance and β portfolios at similar effective levels of ρ.

Computation of $\beta_{s,i}$

Sharpe's β_s in (1) is equivalent to $\delta R_s/\delta R_m$. If we apply a similar differential to (49), and use the unconditional, expected values we obtain:

$$\delta_i R/\delta M = \beta_{s,i} = \beta_i + \gamma_i M \qquad (110)$$

118 / *A New Look at Portfolio Management*

We could, of course, have used just β_i, but this would not have been consistent with the theoretical definition of β_s, nor would it have taken full advantage of the forecasts made available through SDM. Translating Sharpe's β objective function into the terminology of this study:

$$\max R_p - K\dagger \ \beta_p \tag{111}$$

where $\beta_p = \sum_{i=1}^{N} \beta_{s,i}$ and

K† is Sharpe's risk-return trade-off parameter.

Risk Consistency

Equation (111) is linear and can be used as an objective function for the revision algorithm. In order to control for effects of downside risk, however, it is necessary to find a relationship between K† in (111) and K in (103). Equation (103), given $\hat{s}_p$ is intended to be equivalent to:

$$\max R_p - K\hat{s}_p \tag{112}$$

Using (109) and the appropriate variable definitions from this chapter:

$$s_p^2 \approx \beta_p^2 \ s_M^2 \quad \text{or taking square roots*}$$

$$s_p \approx \beta_p \ s_M \tag{113}$$

Substituting (113) into (112), the variance form of the objective function can be written as:

$$\max R_p - (K \ s_M)\beta_p \text{ and setting} \tag{114}$$

* Sharpe and other researchers assume that $\beta_p > 0$ when taking square roots. There is no theoretical justification for this and indeed certain counter-cyclical stocks or portfolios composed of them could have a $\beta_p < 0$. For this reason in the tests conducted in Chapter 5 use the following extension of (113):

$$s_p \approx |\beta_p| s_M$$

$$K\dagger = K\, s_M \qquad (115)$$

will result in similar implicit downside risks for the beta and variance variations on the objective function.

Objective Function

If we define

$$K^\beta_i = {}_iR^c + {}_iD/{}_iP + R_f - f_i - K\, s_M \beta_{s,i} \qquad (116)$$

then (111) with transaction costs and expressed in terms of flow variables becomes:

$$\max \sum_{i=1}^{N} (z_i K^\beta_i - t_i|z_i|) \qquad (117)$$

$$\text{subject to } \sum_{i=1}^{N} z_i = 0$$

Equation (117) is the same form as (106) and consequently the revision algorithm discussed earlier can be employed by changing just the equation to compute K^γ_i to (116) to compute K^β_i.

OBJECTIVE FUNCTION: PRUDENT MAN

In Chapter 2 it is brought to the attention of the reader that the Prudent Man conventions embodied in present laws governing pension fund management are counter to the concepts of portfolio theory. The manager is held responsible for the performance of each asset in the portfolio rather than for the performance of the portfolio as a whole. The SDM Usage Report in Figure 3.17 is an example of this one security at a time approach to portfolio management. Objective functions for this type of criteria need not be strucutred around Beta models, since the overall portfolio characteristics are not a factor in selection. Individual security

120 / *A New Look at Portfolio Management*

distributions can be used directly to build an objective function. Before building single security objective functions, it is necessary to incorporate the level and variance feedback coefficients calculated by (71) and (85) into analysts' subjective, triangular distributions. Beta models must still be constructed to estimate these feedback coefficients.

Feedback Correction: Level

The feedback correction for price return levels can be applied directly to each of the conditional price parameters supplied by the analysts. For the triangular distribution functions described by (40), the three parameters are altered according to:

$$_H P^\dagger_j = a + b \,_H P_j$$

$$_M P^\dagger_j = a + b \,_M P_j \tag{118}$$

$$_L P^\dagger_j = a + b \,_L P_j$$

Substitution of (118) into (43) and (44) yields:

$$\bar{P}^\dagger_j = a + b \,\bar{P}_j \text{ and} \tag{119}$$

$$\sigma^{2c}_{Pj} = b^2 \, \sigma^2_{Pj} \tag{120}$$

Feedback Correction: Variance

Feedback correction to variance is more complex when dealing with triangular distributions directly instead of Beta models with assumed symmetry and homogeneous, independent variance. The SDM triangular distributions are usually not symmetric and the mean and variance of a triangular distribution are not independent. Thus, it is important to avoid the error of altering (119) in the process of further correcting (120) to reflect feedback information. If we define a correction factor k such that:

$$_H P_j^c = {_H P_{\dagger j}} + k$$

$$_M P_j^c = {_M P_{\dagger j}} \tag{121}$$

$$_L P_j^c = {_L P_{\dagger j}} - k$$

then it is apparent from (43), that (119) is unchanged, e.g.

$$\bar{P}^c = ({_H P_{\dagger j}} + k + {_M P_{\dagger j}} + {_L P_{\dagger j}} - k)/3 = \bar{P}\dagger$$

This correction factor does, however, change the variance. In order to implement feedback correction according to (84), we need to find a value for k such that the resulting variance will be equal to the feedback correction factor times the level corrected variance in (120).
In algebraic terms:

$$s_P^c = C\, \sigma_P^{2c} \tag{122}$$

where s_P^c is the price forecast variance corrected for feedback and C is the correction factor computed by (82) (note subscripts for security and environment are not indicated).

Substituting (121) into (44), dropping environment subscripts and collecting terms:

$$s_P^c = k({_H P\dagger} - {_L P\dagger} + k)/6 + \sigma_P^{2c} \tag{123}$$

From (122), therefore:

$$C\sigma_P^{2c} = k(_HP\dagger - {_L}P\dagger + k)/6 + \sigma_P^{2c} \text{ or}$$

$$k^2 + (_HP\dagger - {_L}P\dagger)k + 6(1 - C)\sigma_P^{2c} = 0 \tag{124}$$

Equation (124) is a quadratic in k and by the standard solution to a quadratic equation:

$$k = \frac{-(_HP\dagger - {_L}P\dagger) \pm [(_HP\dagger - {_L}P\dagger)^2 - 24(1 - C)\sigma_P^{2c}]^{\frac{1}{2}}}{2}$$

The proper sign for the square root term can be determined by seeing which sign is consistent with K=0 when no feedback correction is necessary, e.g. C = 1. The equation for k which will result in the same variance correction effect as (82) is, therefore, given by:

$$k = \frac{_LP\dagger - {_H}P\dagger + [(_HP\dagger - {_L}P\dagger)^2 - 24(1 - C)\sigma_P^{2c}]^{\frac{1}{2}}}{2} \tag{125}$$

Examination of (125) shows that when, for example, C < 1, indicating that the subjective variance is too large, K < 0. A negative k will narrow the range of the forecast and thereby reduce the variance consistent with the feedback information. Equation (123) with the value of k computed by (125) provides a value for s_p^c. This variance can then be transformed into price return variance for the ith security by:

$$s_i^2 = \sum_{j=1}^{3} p_j \, V \, {_is_{p_j}^{2c}}/{_iP^2} \tag{126}$$

where V is the horizon adjustment from (32),
$_iP$ is the current price and
p_j is the probability of the j environment.

Objective Function

Now that the parameters of the subjective price distributions have been corrected by feedback information, the Prudent Man objective function can be formulated. In Figure 4.4 the parameters of the price return distribution are defined by:

Figure 4.4. Prudent Man Objective Function Price Return

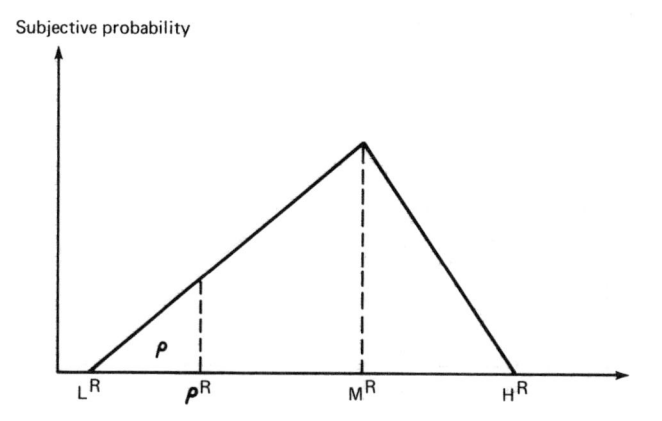

Subjective probability

L^R P^R M^R H^R

P

124 / *A New Look at Portfolio Management*

$$_HR = (_HP^c - P)/12P$$

$$_MR = (_MP^c - P)/12P \text{ and} \tag{127}$$

$$_LR = (_LP^c - P)/12P$$

An objective function, in the same safety first spirit as the functions built for the variance and beta formulations, can be built upon $_\rho R$ in Figure 4.4. If we define:

$$K_i^\rho = {_\rho R_i} + {_iD}/{_iP} - f_i \tag{128}$$

where $_\rho R_i = \sum_{j=1}^{3} p_j \, _\rho R_{i,j}$

then we can expect to fall below K_i^ρ at most ρ of the time. The form of K_i^ρ is, fortunately, similar to K_i^v and K_i^β and can be incorporated directly in an objective function solvable by the revision algorithm. The Prudent Man objective function, therefore, takes the form:

$$\max \sum_{i=1}^{N} (z_i K_i^\rho - t_i|z_i|) \tag{129}$$

$$\text{subject to: } \sum_{i=1}^{N} z_i = 0$$

All that remains before (129) can be solved is to obtain an expression for $_\rho R$ in terms of the parameters given by (127) for each security i in each environment j.

By definition:

$$\rho = \int_{_LR}^{_\rho R} f(\tilde{R}) \, d\tilde{R} \tag{130}$$

A General Pension Fund Management Simulator / 125

where $f(\tilde{R})$ is defined by (40).
Since $f(\tilde{R})$ is not continuously differentiable, two separate cases must be considered depending on whether or not $_\rho R < {_M}R$. When $_\rho R < {_M}R$, it follows by integrating (130) that:

$$_\rho R = {_L}R + (\rho({_H}R - {_L}R)({_M}R - {_L}R))^{\frac{1}{2}} \qquad (131)$$

and when $_\rho R \geq {_M}R$, integration by parts of (130) yields:

$$_\rho R = {_H}R - ((1-\rho)({_H}R^2 - {_L}R{_H}R - {_M}R{_H}R + {_L}R{_M}R))^{\frac{1}{2}} \qquad (132)$$

In practice (131) will almost always be the correct equation. Nevertheless, it is necessary to determine prior to using (131) whether the assumption of $_\rho R < {_M}R$ would be violated. Equation (132) should be used instead of (131) whenever ρ exceeds a value ρ^*. At the critical point:

$\rho^\dagger R = {_M}R$ or using (131)

$$_L R + (\rho^\dagger({_H}R - {_L}R)({_M}R - {_L}R))^{\frac{1}{2}} = {_M}R \qquad (133)$$

Solving for $\rho^\dagger$ yields:

$$\rho^\dagger = ({_M}R - {_L}R)({_H}R - {_L}R) \qquad (134)$$

Therefore, (131) is used to compute ρR unless $\rho > \rho^\dagger$ in which case (132) must be used instead.

Equation (128) can now be evaluated and the mathematics required to solve the revision algorithm with a Prudent Man form for the objective function (129) is complete.

At this point, three variations of portfolio return and risk balancing based on respectively, overall variance, overall responsiveness relative to market changes and individual security decisions have been formulated.

In addition, all three formulations result in a single numerical value for each security. This common structural form permits the use of the same revision algorithm for all three variations. The objective functions treated thus far are representative of the more complex alternatives proposed by researchers. In the following sections, additional objective functions which are more representative of observed management practice are also constructed.

OBJECTIVE FUNCTION: RETURN

Many pension fund managers seek to simply maximize return. They frequently argue in the spirit of the asymmetric Regret function in Figure 3.10 that high returns will "take care of risk" or that while relevant, risk measures are too vague or too unstable to be practical. The return form of the objective function can be viewed as a special case of either the variance or beta functions with the risk parameter K set equal to zero. The return revision algorithm can be stated as:

$$\max \sum_{L=1}^{N} (z_i K_i^R - t_i |z_i|) \qquad (135)$$

$$\text{subject to:} \sum_{L=1}^{N} z_i = 0$$

where $K_i^R = {}_iR^c + {}_iD/{}_iP + R_f - f_i$

Downside risk in this formulation can only be examined *ex post*. Should these evaluations show that the magnitude of the risks is not consistent with Trustor goals, there is, of course, no way to alter investment strategy.

OBJECTIVE FUNCTION: QUALITATIVE

In Chapter 3 all the institutions examined translated numerical return forecasts into qualitative rankings in the general form of buy, neutral or sell classifications. It was also common practice for them to make these qualitative judgments relative to the forecasted market return. In order to

A General Pension Fund Management Simulator / 127

compare decision-making alternatives to current practice, it is necessary to simulate qualitative inputs using the SDM data. Although it would have been preferable to collect rather than to infer qualitative rankings, the managerial barriers to this are reviewed in Chapter 1. The convention in this Chapter is to let the $N-1$ security be the market index. Qualitative classifications can be made according to:

$$\text{Buy if } K_i^R > K_{N-1}^R + G \tag{136}$$

$$\text{Sell if } K_i^R < K_{N-1}^R - G$$

$$\text{Neutral if } K_{N-1}^R - G \leq K_i^R \leq K_{N-1}^R + G$$

where $\pm G$ indicates the band around the market return classified as Neutral.

The qualitative rankings determined by (136) are assigned values according to the following procedure:

$$K_i^Q = 1 \text{ if i is a Buy,}$$

$$K_i^Q = 1 \text{ if i is a Sell and} \tag{137}$$

$$K_i^Q = 0 \text{ if i is Neutral.}$$

The revision algorithm can now be invoked in its familiar form:

$$\max \sum_{i=1}^{N} (z_i K_i^Q - t_i |z_i|) \tag{138}$$

$$\text{subject to: } \sum_{i=1}^{N} z_i = 0$$

Transaction costs are included in (138) to prevent arbitrary buying and selling of Neutral stocks and to provide the revision algorithm with the costs required to balance interperiod cash flows. The values assigned to the K_i^Q will insure that all Buys and Sells are executed subject to upper bound and available cash constraints.

OBJECTIVE FUNCTION: RANDOM

The last variation of the objective function to be considered is random selection. Many economists have stated that random selection of securities, due to the efficiency of the secondary equity markets would generate results as good as those obtained by any formal management system.

The selection in this study is restructed to securities eligible for pension fund investment. Thus, even though risk considerations cannot be formally incorporated into either this objective function or the return and qualitative formulations discussed earlier, the restricted selection universe should reduce any return differentials due to risk factors.

Security parameters for use in the revision algorithm are computed in the following fashion. First, $1/\bar{u} + 2$ integer random numbers between 1 and N inclusive are generated. $\bar{u}$ is the average upper bound for equity securities and the addition of 2 is required for the unlimited upper bounds of the market security and the risk free bond. Then for each security i:

$$K_i^N = \begin{cases} 1. \text{ if } i \in \{\text{Random integers}\} \\ 0. \text{ if } i \notin \{\text{Random integers}\} \end{cases} \tag{139}$$

The revision algorithm becomes:

$$\max \sum_{i=1}^{N} (z_i K_i^N - t_i |z_i|) \tag{140}$$

$$\text{subject to: } \sum_{i=1}^{N} (z_i = 0$$

Random sells need not be generated, since securities in the portfolio for which $K_i^N = 0$ will be sold to provide funds to purchase the securities for

Figure 4.5. General Flow Chart

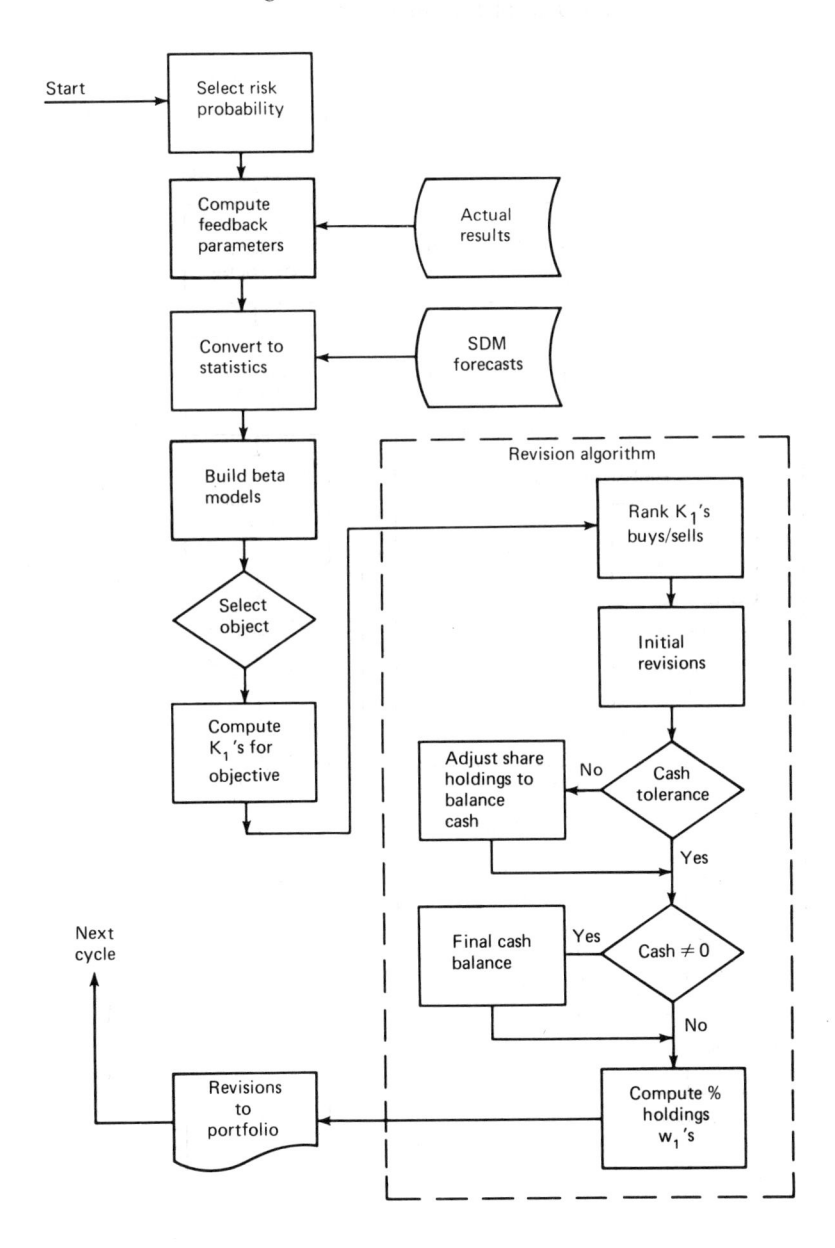

which $K_1^N = 1$. Should a security be selected for two or more consecutive periods, a transaction cost saving will accrue to the portfolio.

SUMMARY

The three major areas developed in this chapter are: 1) the conversion of SDM forecasts and feedback statistics into input parameters for a portfolio management model, 2) the structure of a low cost portfolio revision model which includes diversification constraints, transaction costs and management fees and 3) the formulation of six alternative objective functions which reflect important management issues and alternatives in pension fund management. A summary flow chart of these components and their interrelationships is given in Figure 4.5.

As stated in the outset of this chapter, the goal of the process shown in Figure 4.5 is to generate portfolio management decisions which are at least as good as those which would have been generated by portfolio managers operating under the same management information systems, goals and constraints. The process developed is also constructive, in the sense that if certain configurations appear to be effective management strategies, the tools employed in the evaluations may also be used to implement the process. The process shown in Figure 4.5 forms the basis in the next chapter for testing various hypotheses concerning the effectiveness of alternative methods for pension fund management.

Chapter 5

Evaluation of Alternative Decision-Making Systems

INTRODUCTION

In Chapter 1, the focus of the analysis was directed toward the Decision component in Figure 1.2. This component contains the interaction of portfolio goals and management information systems through which security forecasts are converted into portfolio decisions. In this chapter a number of hypotheses are tested concerning the form of this interaction and its relevance to future academic research and management applications.

The procedure to evaluate each alternative combination of goals and systems is the same and follows the steps outlined below.

1. *Formulate Hypotheses.* Constructing hypotheses such as—Feedback correction of forecasts improves performance; or—Portfolios revised according to portfolio theory significantly differ from those managed according to traditional, one security at a time, qualitative methods—is the first step in the process..

2. *Build Systems.* Given the hypotheses from step 1, the second step is to build from the models developed in Chapter 4 the appropriate management systems which represent the alternatives in each hypothesis. All management systems, however, are in the general form shown in Figure 4.5.

3. *Simulate Decision Behavior.* Once the hypotheses have been translated into mathematical systems, each system begins with the same initial cash contribution and manages it using the SDM forecasts over the period January 1970 through October 1971. Cash contributions and withdrawals are identical for all management simulations and follow a common pattern for new pension funds. New securities do appear on the approved list during the simulation and a number of securities available at the beginning are dropped during the simulation. Should any of the latter be held by a portfolio when they are deleted from the approved investment list, they will be sold the following month.

4. *Measure Performance.* During the simulations in step 3, fund performance is measured in two important dimensions. First, the return on the funds under management is computed for each monthly decision cycle. At the completion of the simulation, these monthly returns provide the data to compute overall Bank Administration Institute return and to test for significant differences in returns between alternative management systems. Secondly, the decisions made are compared to those which would have been made under conditions of perfect knowledge for the coming month. Alternative systems may then be compared relative to their departure from a common standard of perfect knowledge.

5. *Test Hypotheses.* The final step is to use the return and decision data generated during the simulations to determine whether or not significant differences exist between alternative management systems.

Although it would have been desirable to examine the interaction of various system parameters and management goals using, for example, a two-way analysis of variance design with interaction, the cost required to generate sufficient data for this test greatly exceeded available research funds. By a careful selection of hypotheses, however, certain interactions relevant to the selection of pension management systems can be evaluated by the statistical hypothesis testing tools introduced later in this chapter.

DATA

Source

The data used in this study were provided by one of the major institutions in the field of pension fund management and represents a unique collection of anticipations data. In fact, when one considers the amount of funds managed by this bank in conjunction with the concentration statistics cited in Chapter 2, this data formed the basis for approximately 3 percent of all trades on the New York Stock Exchange during the January 1970 through November 1971 analysis period. The data were collected under controlled conditions through the SDM process described in Chapter 3.

Even though the data were used daily by the bank and, therefore, edited and controlled on a routine basis, initial simulation tests revealed several dozen, unusually large anticipated returns on the order of $\pm$ 50 percent or even more per month. Subsequent investigation showed that in these cases, analysts had either neglected to correct their yearly forecasts for stock dividends or splits until after the date of record or had changed them prior to this date. In SDM, the yearly vs monthly return horizon makes this error difficult to catch, particularly for stock dividends less than 100 percent. When caught, the timing error was corrected for the next monthly report, but this correction was, apparently, not made to current or past report data. Consequently, all 232 common stocks in the universe were individually checked against Moody's Dividend Record [56] for 1969, 1970, 1971 and 1972 and all forecasts were corrected, if necessary, to reflect stock splits or stock dividends in excess of 5 percent. This control process is indicative of the additional complexities incurred when management systems are built around anticipatory subjective data in addition to *ex post* accounting data. The common stock universe of 232 securities was selected from over 400 securities included at least once in SDM during the twenty-two month period. The selection criteria was that at least twelve months of continuous forecasts were to be available. During the test period, the bank itself realized that many of the stocks in SDM were special situations not approved for general pension fund investment and might be in the system for only a few months. At the end of the test period, the bank had reduced its SDM approved list to under 200 securities. As a result of both the bank's actions and the author's desire to have at least twelve observations for all feedback evaluations, the universe varies from 202 at the beginning, to 232 during the middle of the test period, to 189 at the end.

Economic Conditions

The simulation tests are made over a time during which the stock market and the economy went through essentially a complete cycle. This can be seen by referring to Figure 5.1 and noting that average monthly return, including dividends, for the DOW Jones Index over this period

134 / *A New Look at Portfolio Management*

Figure 5.1. Economic Conditions

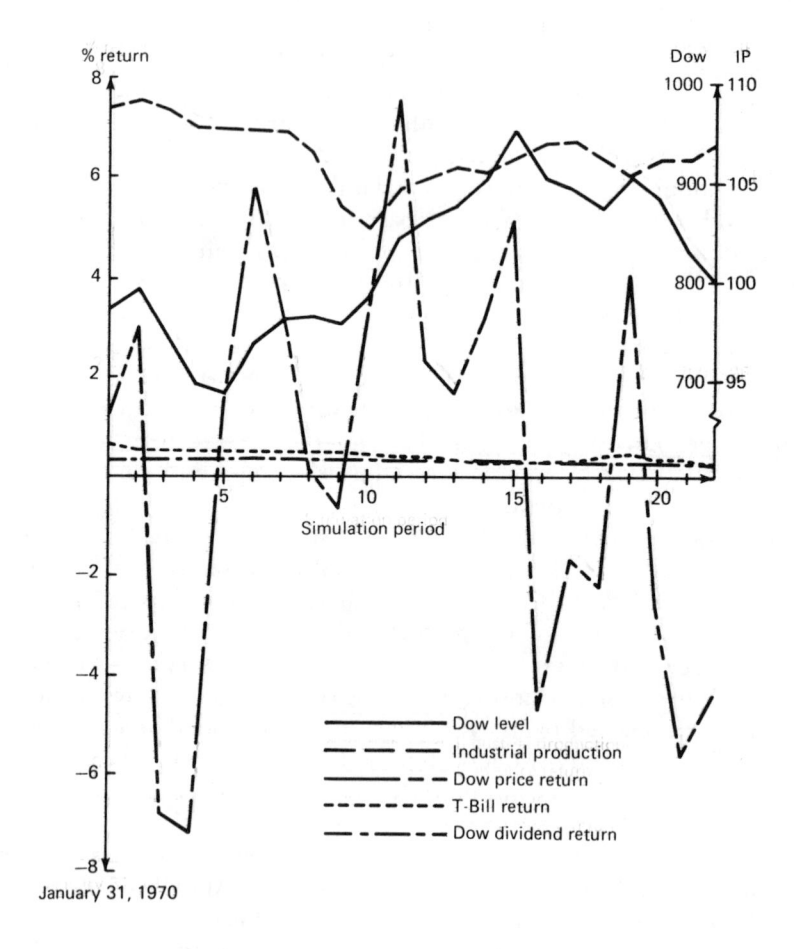

was only .65 percent. When the average dividend return of 33 percent is subtracted from this figure, the monthly price return is seen to be .32 percent or a nominal growth rate of just 3.84 percent a year.

During this time economic activity, as measured by the Index of Industrial Production, fell for the first ten months and began a gradual recovery to beginning levels with intermittent dips over the next thirteen months. Interest rates during the first fourteen months continued their decline from historic highs in 1969 to more normal levels and fluctuated only slightly during the remainder of the simulation period.

The absence of strong trends in the economy in conjuction with large monthly variations affords an excellent framework to evaluate the decision-making efficiency of alternative management systems. Results should not be biased by economic trends while the large monthly fluctuations place a premium on effective decision-making and make differences in the effectiveness of processes much easier to detect.

Transaction Costs

The bank, as part of the support for this research analyzed its total equity purchases and associated commissions over a representative three-month period. Transactions covered those made through regular exchanges, block transfers, over-the-counter and all special arrangements. The overall commission costs as a percentage of the dollar volume transacted were .37 percent, .39 percent and .38 percent. Consequently, the commision component of transaction costs for equity securities in this research is assumed to be .4 percent. Traders, however, were quick to point out that effective transaction costs should also include the effect of adverse markets movements caused by trading. Estimates for this component ranged from 0 percent for a passive strategy to as high as 10 percent for an active, short duration program. Although this cost should vary with the thinness of the market for each security, and the algorithms developed in the preceding chapter are formulated to handle individual security transaction costs, the traders questioned did not feel able to supply this date for every security. They did agree, however, that a general estimate of 2 percent of the price of equity securities for adverse market movement, considering the size and timing of the usual bank transaction, would be reasonable.

Consequently, the transaction cost for securities is estimated to be 2 percent for adverse market movement plus .4 percent commission costs for a total of 2.4 percent.

In order to test the Wells Fargo market fund approach, a security representing the Dow Jones Index is incorporated in the general model in Chapter 4. Due to the thickness of the market for the stocks in this index and the possibility of substitution, the assumption is made that adverse market movement can be avoided.* The assumed transaction cost for the market stock, therefore, is just .4 percent.

Technically, there is no commission involved when a large bank purchases 30-day T-Bills. A nominal spread for the dealer, however, would be on the order of ⅛ percent or less. The assumed transaction cost for T-Bills, therefore, is .1 percent and, due to the depth of he T-Bill market, no adverse market movement effect is included.

Initial simulation tests revealed a rapid turnover in portfolio holdings. This is not surprising in light of the wide swings in market return shown in Figure 5.1 and the resulting unstabling effects on analysts' forecasts. Although turnover in practice was not this large, the holding period estimate required by the revision algorithm should be consistent with turnover in portfolios as managed by this algorithm. The initial estimate for the average holding period, therefore, was set at two months.

Contributions and Withdrawals

The same representative fund is used for all simulation tests. Cash flows in and out of the fund are shown in Table 5.1 below.

The pattern of cash flows has been set to be consistent with likely corporate treasurer behavior over the economic cycle shown in Figure 5.1. During the first part of the simulation, interest rates are still high and production is falling. Opportunity costs for corporate funds are, therefore, also high and pension obligations are likely to be met by fund withdrawals. During the second half, interest rates are lower, production is climbing and corporate cash should be easier, thereby prompting treasurers to fund long-term pension obligations. It is beyond the scope of this research to review the actuarial planning necessary to determine required funding or to examine the many variations in pensions plans. The interested reader is referred to the comprehensive series by Bankers Trust Company [14].

*The similarity between movements in the DOW and the Standard and Poor 425 indicies suggests that DOW return behavior may be achieved without actually holding the stocks in the DOW index.

Table 5.1.

Period	Contributions Each Period	Withdrawals Each Period
1	$10,000,000.00	$ 0.00
2–9	0.00	50,000.00
10–12	0.00	0.00
13–22	50,000.00	0.00

Management Fees

During the first quarter of 1971, the bank which supplied the data for this study conducted a private survey of pension fund management fees. For all nine banks in the survey, fees decreased with the size of the fund, with the average annual fee for a ten million dollar account approximately .09 percent of the fund's value at year end. The resulting fee of $9,000 for an account of this magnitude also exceeded the minimum fee for all banks in the survey. The average fee for accounts 100 million and over was .06 percent. Following the removal of price controls in 1974, however, it is likely that the .09 percent used in this study for a ten million dollar account, although appropriate for the simulation period, is probably 30 percent or more below current fee levels. The management fee for the market fund security must, of course, be an estimate of the price corporate treasurers would be willing to pay for this service and the mark-up over operating costs necessary to induce the banks to offer it. An estimate of .03 percent, in the author's opinion, should provide revenues to encourage banks. The management fee for 30-day T-Bills should be nominal. In this study, the management fee for 30-day T-Bills has been set by the author at .01 percent. Although it is not current practice to have differential fees for various security risk classes, at this level, banks should be more than compensated for operational expenses while corporations would not be charged for risk management when, in fact, the risk of loss is not present.

Although the remainder of this chapter is not overly mathematical, the managerially oriented reader may wish to skip to the end of the chapter for a summary of results and management inplications.

PERFORMANCE MEASURES

Return

Figure 5.2 illustrates the cash flow and timing considerations in the computation of monthly returns. Solid horizontal lines represent the passage of time, while the dashed lines indicate instantaneous time. Dividends, for example, are assumed to be received at the end of the month on stocks held during the preceding month. All cash contributions or withdrawals are assumed to occur at the beginning of the month. Although corrections to account for flows within periods are frequently

FIGURE 5.2

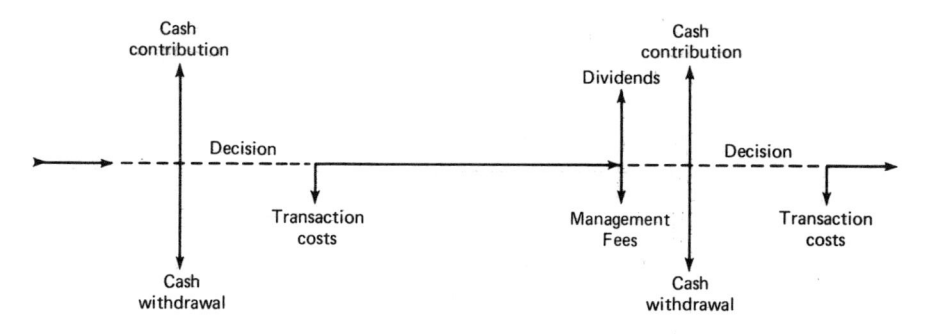

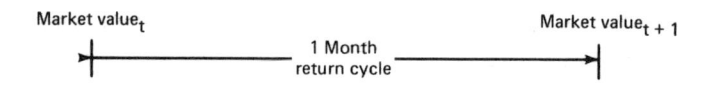

```
    Cash                              Cash
contribution                      contribution
                      Dividends
         Decision                         Decision
────────┼──────────────┬──────────────┼──────────┬────────
         │             │              │          │
         │       Transaction      Management  Transaction
         │          costs            Fees        costs
       Cash                          Cash
    withdrawal                    withdrawal


Market value_t                    Market value_{t+1}
  ├──────────── 1 Month ────────────┤
              return cycle
```

made for quarterly or yearly periods, the monthly frequency in this research would make such adjustments an unnecessary complication.

Monthly, *ex post*, portfolio return is computed according to:

$$_tR_p = \frac{\text{Market Value}_{t+1} - \text{Market Value}_t}{\text{Market Value}_t} \qquad (141)$$

Average monthly return over a T month simulation is given by:

$$\bar{R}_p = \sum_{t=1}^{T} {}_tR_p/T \quad \text{and} \qquad (142)$$

the variance of monthly return follows directly as:

$$V_p = \sum_{i=1}^{T} ({}_tR_p - \bar{R}_p)^2/(T-1) \qquad (143)$$

A time weighted annual rate of return analogous to the Bank Administration Institute measure is also computed for each complete simulation run. Since all periods are assumed to be equal length months, this return is computed by:

$$B_p = (\prod_{t=1}^{T} (1 + {}_tR_p))^{\frac{12}{T}} - 1 \qquad (144)$$

The limited span of the simulation unfortunately does not make it practical to compute any variance estimate for this performance measure.

Dispersion

Although the return performance measures discussed above provide a convenient way to compare alternative systems, by themselves they may be misleading. Two portfolios, for example, may have similar returns yet differ widely in composition or alternatively have similar compositions and yet widely divergent returns. The Dispersion Index defined in this section measures the difference in composition between two portfolios, a and b and is defined as:

$$D_t = \frac{\sum_{i=1}^{N} (_tw_i^a - _tw_i^b)^2}{\sum_{i=1}^{N} (_tw_i^a)^2 + \sum_{i=1}^{N} (_tw_i^b)^2} \quad (145)$$

where

$_tw_i^j$ = percent of portfolio j in security i at time t
N = maximum number of securities in the approved universe

If portfolios a and b at time t contain no securities in common, then $D_t = 1$. On the other hand, if a and b are identical, the $D_t = 0$.

As an example, consider the case when two portfolios have a common upper bound of .05 on all holdings and out of twenty securities held in each portfolio, five are held in common. Then according to (145),

$$D_t = \frac{15(.05)^2 + 15(.05)^2 + 5(0)^2}{20(.05)^2 + 20(.05)^2} \quad \text{or}$$

$$D_t = .75$$

In this case D_t has a straight forward interpretation, e.g. 75 percent of the holdings are different.

A complementary measure to D_t, is the selection index defined by:

$$S_t = 100(1. - D_t) \quad (146)$$

where S_t measures percent similarity between portfolios.
In the example above:

$$S_t = 100(1. - .75) = 25\%$$

indicating a 25 percent overlap between a and b.

The principal advantage of D_t and S_t over simple counting procedures, which could have been used in the example, is that these measures can also be computed when upper bounds are unequal, holdings are not at their upper bounds and portfolio sizes differ.

This research study uses D_t and S_t to measure correspondence between all portfolios generated and those portfolios arrived at using perfect knowledge of future returns. Thus when the D_t's for two portfolios are compared, this comparison is not primarily an evaluation of whether they have different compositions, but whether one is closer than the other to the decisions which would have been made if the future were known with certainty. This approach was taken to provide a common standard against which changes in composition due to different management systems could be analyzed.

STATISTICAL TESTS

Performance Measures

Statistical comparison of the differences between, for example, the average monthly returns for two alternative management systems cannot be done using a simple test of differences between two means since the observations are not independent. It is possible, however, to construct a test statistic in terms of the difference between returns in each month which avoids the correlated observation problem. Winer [80] has shown that if the economic condition and management system effects on monthly returns or dispersions are assumed to be independent, then:

$$t = \frac{\bar{d} - (\mu_a - \mu_b)}{(s_d^2/n)^{1/2}} \qquad (147)$$

where $\bar{d}$ is the mean of the n differences between monthly performance measures, s_d^2 is the variance of d, μ_a is the true mean for system a, μ_b is the true mean for system b and t is a test statistic having a student's t distribution with n−1 degrees of freedom.

When the standard computation formulas for s_d^2 are $\bar{d}$ are substituted into (147) along with the null hypothesis formulation, i.e. $\mu_a = \mu_b$, we obtain:

$$t = \frac{\sum_{i=1}^{n} d_i/n}{\left(\left(n\sum_{i=1}^{n} d_i^2 - \left(\sum_{i=1}^{n} d_i\right)^2\right) \middle/ n(n-1)\right)^{1/2} \middle/ n^{1/2}} \quad \text{or}$$

$$t = \frac{\sum_{i=1}^{n} d_i}{\left(\left(n\sum_{i=1}^{n} d_i^2 - \left(\sum_{i=1}^{n} d_i\right)^2\right) \middle/ (n-1)\right)^{1/2}} \quad \text{and} \quad (148)$$

d_i = Performance Measure for system a in period i
− Performance Measure for system b in period i

Winer also points out that if the performance measures are positively correlated between systems, which they should be in this research design, the magnitude of s_d^2 will be reduced as this correlation increases, thus making the hypothesis testing procedure more efficient.

Although the return and dispersion measures may themselves depart from normality in the extremes, the use of differences should, due to the effect of the central limit theorem, also increase the robustness of the necessary normality assumption for the d_i's.

Composition

Another way of comparing the composition of two portfolios is to compute the probability that if a security is held in portfolio a it will also be held by portfolio b during the same period. This approach has been taken by Sharpe [63] to compare portfolios generated by his diagonal model with those generated using only volatility as measured by β. Based on a

144 / A New Look at Portfolio Management

sixty-three security universe during thirty selection periods with twenty securities included in each portfolio, Sharpe's data indicates that if a security were selected by the complete diagonal model there was a 92.8 percent chance it would also be selected by the much simpler β algorithm. Although Sharpe did not test the significance of his results, visual inspection lead him to conclude:

> As always, generalization may be dangerous. But at least in this instance, average return and volatility appear to have captured enough of the historical record to serve adequately for portfolio analysis subject to reasonably stringent upper bounds.

Mathematically this approach to the analysis of differences in portfolio composition can be expressed as:

$$\Pr(_tw_i^b > \underline{w} \mid {_tw_i^a} > \underline{w}) \geq \alpha, \quad i=1,\ldots,N \quad \text{and} \quad t=1,\ldots,T \tag{149}$$

where $\underline{w}$ is the minimum percentage considered to be a significant holding and α is the overall probability that if a security is held in significant amounts by portfolio a, that it will also be held in significant amounts by portfolio b.

If we define variables $_ty_i$ and $_tx_i$ such that:

$$_ty_i = \begin{cases} 1 & \text{if } {_tw_i^a} \geq \underline{w} \\ 0 & \text{if } {_tw_i^a} < \underline{w} \end{cases} \quad \text{and}$$

$$_tx_i = \begin{cases} 1 & \text{if } {_tw_i^b} \geq \underline{w} | {_ty_i} = 1 \\ 0 & \text{otherwise} \end{cases}$$

then the sample estimate of α can be computed by:

$$\hat{\alpha} = \frac{\sum_{t=1}^{T} \sum_{i=1}^{N} {_tx_i}}{\sum_{t=1}^{T} \sum_{i=1}^{N} {_ty_i}} = \frac{X}{Y}$$

In this context α can be interpreted as a binomial probability, and, as shown in Siegel [65], a test to determine whether or not $\hat{\alpha}$ significantly differs from a hypothesized value α is given by:

$$z = \frac{(X \pm .5) - \alpha Y}{(Y \alpha (1-\alpha))^{1/2}} \quad (150)$$

where for large Y, z is a standard normal deviate and the $\pm$ .5 is a continuity correction necessary when using the normal deviate, e.g., when $X < \alpha Y$, .5 is added to X and when $X > \alpha Y$, .5 is subtracted from X.

In this study, if $\hat{\alpha}$ is not significantly less than 90 percent at the 5 percent level, the portfolios are interpreted as being essentially the same. When this test is applied to Sharpe's results, $\hat{\alpha}$ is significantly greater than 90 percent at the 1 percent as well as the 5 percent level.

Since the selection of $\alpha = 90$ percent as a criteria for similarity, although chosen to be similar to Sharpe's judgment, is still arbitrary, (150) is solved for α in terms of a critical level for z. In this way, given the simulation results, it is possible to say at what level of α the null hypothesis would just fail to be rejected. Letting $z^{\dagger}$ represent the critical value for z, it follows from (150) that

$$\alpha = \frac{2X + z^{\dagger 2} + ((2X + z^{\dagger 2})^2 - 4(Y + z^{\dagger 2}) X^2/Y)^{1/2}}{2(Y + z^{\dagger 2})} \quad (151)$$

A significance level of 5 percent corresponds to a value of -1.645 for $z^{\dagger}$. Again using Sharpe's results, the hypothesized value for α would have to exceed 94.3 percent before Sharpe's hypothesis that the two algorithms were generating essentially equivalent portfolios could be rejected at the 5 percent level.

HYPOTHESIS FORMULATION AND TESTING

Test Strategy

The models developed in Chapter 4 permit a wide variety of management systems and goals to be structured and simulated. Even without considering different parameter values, for example, changing the esti-

146 / A New Look at Portfolio Management

mated holding period from two to three or four months, there are over 160 plausible structural combinations. When significant variations in parameter values are added to structural alternatives, the number of possible systems quickly climbs into the thousands. In order to deal with this large array of systems, a three step testing strategy is followed. First, all parameters are set to values as representative as possible of observed pension fund management practice. Secondly, hypotheses concerning the major structural issues facing executive management are formulated, translated into models, simulated over the test period and statistically evaluated. Finally, the robustness of selected results is examined by varying certain parameter values.

Initial Parameter Values

Table 5.2 contains the name of the parameter, the chapter and equation in which the parameter was first introduced, the algebraic symbol, the initial representative value and a comment or reference to an earlier discussion to support the initial value chosen.

Hypothesis Formulation

The variety in possible structural forms makes it advantageous to have a convenient way to specify different system configurations. Possible structural dimensions along with variations in each dimension are listed in Table 5.3. A system, for example, which had an objective function risk adjusted by variance, and a management information system using triangular distribution inputs, linear market models, all feedback correction features and strict upper bound limits would be coded as:

$$O - V,$$
$$F - T,$$
$$R - L,$$
$$C - MLV,$$
$$U - N.$$

The upper bound violation dimension in the example above is an option in the computer program version of the revision algorithm which avoids selling a security if it exceeds its upper bound due to price fluctuations. This option was added to the algorithm to permit testing the effect of soft vs hard upper bounds.

Table 5.4 contains the major hypotheses addressed by this study concerning the design of pension fund management systems. Each hypothesis is numbered for reference in the next section on experimental results. Within each hypothesis the two alternative systems are specified in terms of the structural codes given in Table 5.3. Finally, the relevant performance measure for each hypothesis is identified.

The hypotheses in Table 5.4 were selected for their relevance to the management policy issues raised in Chapters 2 and 3 and important assumptions in portfolio management theory. The hypotheses have also been cast in a form which supports generally held views. Failure to reject any hypothesis would confirm these views, while rejection would discredit them.

Hypotheses Evaluation

Table 5.5 contains the experimental results for the hypotheses formulated in Table 5.4. The first column indicates the hypothesis number while the second specifies the test statistic. The direction of the hypothesis is given in the third column. In the first hypothesis, for example, system b is hypothesized to produce higher returns than system a or $\mu_a < \mu_b$. Consequently, since all tests are on the basis of $\mu_a - \mu_b$, a "$-$" is in the third column.* The fourth column contains the value of the test statistic, which has the same algebraic sign as the difference between the performance measure means. The percentage in the fifth column is the Type I error significance level or the probability of being incorrect if the hypothesis as stated in Table 5.4 is rejected. The sixth and last columns contain respectively, the direct inference from the experiment and possible managerial implications. Additional experimental results are presented in later sections. The focus of this research, however, can be found in the last column of Table 5.5.

Portfolio Performance

The emphasis thus far has been on examining the relative impact on peformance of changes in management system structure and parameters. Since decisions by the bank for actual pension funds were, for proprietary reasons, not part of this study, it is not possible to draw a comparison between what the bank actually achieved with the SDM forecasts and what

---

* All inequalities imply a one tail test, while equalities imply a two tail test.

Table 5.2.

Initial Parameter Values

Parameter	Eqn	Symbol	Value	Comment (Reference)
Maximum Universe	89	N	234	Includes market fund and T-Bills.
Simulation Periods	142	T	22	Complete market and economic cycle.
Equity Trans. Cost	92	t_1	2.4%	Market effect plus brokerage.
Market Fund Trans. Cost	92	t_{N-1}	.4%	No market effect assumed.
T-Bill Trans. Cost	92	t_N	.1%	Nominal.
Holding Period	---	---	2	Empirical observation.
Estimated Overall Transaction Cost	108	T_e	2.4%	Initial portfolio all cash. This estimate is revised each period by the revision algorithm to equal the overall transaction cost percentage for the prior period.
Equity Management Fee	93	f_1	.09%	Representative.
Market Fund Management	93	f_{N-1}	.03%	Marketable.
T-Bill Management Fee	93	f_N	.01%	Nominal.
Equity Upper Bound	100	u_1	5%	Balance between effective diversification to satisfy Prudent Man requirements and ability to achieve performance in excess of the market.

Market Fund Upper Bound	100	u_{N-1}	100%	Market Fund is assumed to be adequately diversified to meet Prudent Man restrictions.
T-Bill Upper Bound	100	u_N	100%	All funds may be prudently invested in T-Bills if equity market prospects are poor.
Risk Probability	101	ρ	15.87%	Author's estimate. Lower values of ρ cause the revision algorithm to select primarily T-Bills. This would be inconsistent with observed management behavior during the same period. This value also corresponds to a value of 1 standard deviation for K in
Composition Similarity	148	α	90%	Consistent with Sharpe's implicit α.
Neutral Band for Qualitative Judgments	136	G	.83%	Equivalent to 10 percent a year on either side of the market. Similar to observed values in practice and not so large as to prohibit all equity portfolios in any of the test periods.
Length of Moving Average With Data Age Equivalent to Feedback Coefficients	33	J	12	Analysts' used a twelve-month horizon to forecast SDM data and were evaluated with a twelve-month lag.

150 / *A New Look at Portfolio Management*

Table 5.3.

Structural Codes

Structural Dimension	Code	Variation		Chapter 4 Equation Reference	Code
Objective Function	O	Variance Beta Volatility Single Stock Return Not Risk Adjusted Qualitative Random Selection		104 116 128 135 137 139	V B S R Q N
Equity Forecast Form	F	Most Likely Point Estimate Triangular Distribution None		40 43 —	M T N
Return Estimation	R	Single Stock Linear Market Model Quadratic Market Model None		127 57 57 —	S L Q N
Feedback* Correction	C	Market & Equities	Variance Only Level Only Level & Variance	85,125 78,118 78,118	MV ML MLV
		Equities	Variance Only Level Only Level & Variance	85,125 78,118 78,118	EV EL ELV
		None		—	N
Upper Bound Violation	U	Yes No		— —	Y N

*Note feedback correction for single stock selection does require either a linear or quadratic beta model to compute feedback coefficients. Depending on which is used, an L or a Q respectively will be appended to the feedback code.

Table 5.4.
Formulation of Hypotheses

No	Alt	Hypothesis	O	F	R	C	U	Measure
1	a	Given the same value for ρ, single stock selection systems (such as SDM) should overstate downside portfolio risks and, therefore, generate	S	T	S	MLVQ	N	$\bar{R}_p$
	b	less return than portfolios managed according to portfolio theory.	V	T	Q	MLV	N	
2	a	The composition of portfolios selected by single stock selection systems should be further away from the optimal, given perfect knowledge,	S	T	S	MLVQ	N	$\bar{D}_p$
	b	than the composition of portfolios determined according to portfolio theory.	V	T	Q	MLV	N	
3	a	The composition of portfolios selected by single stock selection systems should differ	S	T	S	MLVQ	N	$\hat{\alpha}$
	b	widely from those established according to portfolio theory.	V	T	Q	MLV	N	

Table 5.4. (continued)

Formulation of Hypotheses

No	Alt	Hypothesis	O	F	R	C	U	Measure
4	a	Due to such things as market efficiency, transactions costs, etc., single stock selection systems	S	T	S	MLVQ	N	$\bar{R}_p$
	b	should not generate returns significantly different from randomly selected portfolios.	N	N	N	N	N	
5	a	Consistent with hypothesis 4, single stock selection systems should not differ any more in composition from optimal, given perfect knowledge,	S	T	S	MLVQ	N	$\bar{D}_p$
	b	than randomly selected portfolios.	N	N	N	N	N	
6	a	Single stock selection systems incorporating risk adjusted returns should generate lower returns than	S	T	S	MLVQ	N	$\bar{R}_p$
	b	systems which maximize returns without considering a risk adjustment.	R	T	Q	EL	N	
7	a	The assumption made in Chapter 1, that quantitative forecasting systems, such as SDM, would generate higher returns	S	T	S	MLVQ	N	$\bar{R}_p$
	b	with better risk control than qualitative systems, is true.	Q	M	L	N	N	

8	a	Sharpe implied that the similar compositions generated by his diagonal, variance model and	V	T	Q	ELV	N	$\bar{R}_p$
	b	beta, responsiveness model would result in similar performance. Sharpe's inference is presumed to be true.	B	T	Q	MLV	N	
9	a	Consistent with hypothesis 8, the composition of portfolios generated by Sharpe's diagonal model will not differ from optimal, perfect knowledge portfolios,	V	T	Q	ELV	N	$\bar{D}_p$
		any more than portfolios generated by Sharpe's beta model.	B	T	Q	ELV	N	
10	a	Replication of Sharpe's comparison between diagonal model portfolios and	V	T	Q	ELV	N	$\hat{\alpha}$
	b	beta model portfolios should confirm his observation of similarity. Sophisticated systems which employ feedback correction to management market forecasts as well as to analysts' conditional equity fore-	B	T	Q	ELV	N	
11	a	casts will generate higher returns than systems	V	T	Q	MLV	N	$\bar{R}_p$
	b	which correct only analyst's forecasts.	V	T	Q	ELV	N	

Table 5.4. (continued)
Formulation of Hypotheses

No	Alt	Hypothesis	O	F	R	C	U	Measure
12	a	Systems which do not correct management's market forecasts, but which do correct analysts' forecasts for level and variance will generate higher returns than	V	T	Q	ELV	N	$\bar{R}_p$
	b	similar systems which correct analysts' forecasts only for level.	V	T	Q	EL	N	
13	a	Systems which do not correct management's market forecasts, but which do correct analyst's forecasts for level will generate higher returns than	V	T	Q	EL	N	$\bar{R}_p$
	b	similar systems which have no feedback correction at all.	V	T	Q	N	N	
14	a	A beta portfolio management system based on a quadratic beta model will outperform	B	T	Q	ELV	N	$\bar{R}_p$
	b	a similar portfolio management system using only linear beta models.	B	T	L	ELV	N	
15	a	Diagonal models which include skewness in the form of non-linear, beta models and the use of possibly skewed triangular distributions will outperform	V	T	Q	ELV	N	$\bar{R}_p$
	b	diagonal models which are restricted to linear beta models and most likely, point estimate forecasts.	V	M	L	ELV	N	

16	a	If the level of the risk probability is lowered from 15.87 percent to	V	T	Q	ELV	N	$\bar{R}_p$ N
	b	10 percent, return will fall as well since higher return, but riskier stocks are eliminated.	V	T	Q	ELV	N	$\bar{R}_p$ N
17	a	If the risk level is lowered from 15.87 percent to	V	T	Q	ELV	N	$\bar{R}_p$ N
	b	2.5 percent return will fall as well, since higher return but riskier stocks are eliminated.	V	T	Q	ELV	N	$\bar{R}_p$ N
18	a	If for portfolio-based systems the risk level is lowered from 2.5 percent to	V	T	Q	ELV	N	$\bar{R}_p$ N
	b	.1 percent return will fall as riskier stocks are eliminated. This hypothesis is to confirm the robustness of 17.	V	T	Q	ELV	N	
19	a	The behavior of return will be the same for single stock selection systems as for the diagonal models in 16 and 17 when risk is lowered from 15.87 percent	S	T	S	MLVQ	N	$\bar{R}_p$ N
	b	to .1 percent.	S	T	S	MLVQ	N	
20	a	For single stock selection systems without feedback correction, return will fall as the risk level is lowered from 2.5 percent to	S	T	S	N	N	$\bar{R}_p$ N
	b	.1 percent. This hypothesis is to confirm the robutness of 19 for single stock systems without feedback.	S	T	S	N	N	

Table 5.4. (continued)
Formulation of Hypotheses

No	Alt	Hypothesis	O	F	R	C	U	Measure
21	a	Systems with hard upper bounds will produce lower returns than	S	T	S	ELVQ	N	$\bar{R}_p$
	b	systems with soft upper bounds which do not automatically sell securities to meet upper bound limits.	S	T	S	ELVQ	Y	
22	a	Systems with hard upper bounds as in 21a, but without any feedback correction and with risk at .1 percent vs 15.87 percent will produce lower returns than	S	T	S	N	N	$\bar{R}_p$
	b	similar systems with soft upper bounds. This hypothesis is to confirm the robustness of 21.	S	T	S	N	Y	
23	a	At a low risk level of 2.5 percent single stock selection systems with analyst feedback on level and variance will outperform	S	T	S	ELVQ	N	$\bar{R}_p$
	b	similar systems without any analyst feedback correction.	S	T	S	N	N	
24	a	At a low level of risk of .1 percent single stock selection systems with analyst and management feedback will outperform similar systems with	S	T	S	MLVQ	N	$\bar{R}_p$
	b	no feedback. This hypothesis is to confirm the robustness of 23.	S	T	S	N	N	

Table 5.5.

Evaluation of Hypotheses

No	s	d	Value	Sig	Inference	Management Implications
1	t	–	+.78	78%	*Contrary* to the hypothesis, single stock systems do *not* generate lower returns and, indeed, the single stock systems could be said, with just a 22 percent Type I error, to generate higher returns than the portfolio approach.	Traditional, one stock at a time management systems may be superior to normative portfolio management schemes proposed by the academic community.
2	t	+	-.47	68%	*Contrary* to the hypothesis, single stock systems are *not* further away from perfect knowledge results. If the 3rd and 4th periods were not in the sample, single stock systems would have been significantly closer.	Consistent with 1, it may be possible for pension funds managers to manage one stock at a time and still do as well, without violating prudent man norms, as by using portfolio management approaches.
3	z	–	-26.	0%	The hypothesis is strongly *supported* by the data; portfolio composition differs widely between the single stock, SDM approach and the portfolio approach.	The conclusions drawn in 1 and 2 are not the result of a small percentage of the securities held accounting for the differences, but are due to significantly different compositions.

158 / *A New Look at Portfolio Management*

Table 5.5. (continued)

No	s	d	Value	Sig	Inference	Management Implications
4	t	0	+3.78	.01%	*Contrary* to the hypothesis, there is a highly significant difference favoring SDM type systems over random selection.	Market efficiency, transaction costs and fees do not seem to preclude better than randomly generated returns. Thus it would appear that pension fund managers can legitimately refute the dart board characterization placed upon them.
5	t	0	−2.68	.015%	*Contrary* to the hypothesis, there is a highly significant difference between single stock and randomly selected portfolios in terms of their conformance with optimal, perfect knowledge selection. Single stock portfolios are clearly closer to optimal.	Further reinforcement of 4 to include the composition of the portfolio as well as return performance. Random portfolios had about the same level of variance as single stock portfolios, but had negative returns 78 percent more of the time.
6	t	—	+.39	65%	*Contrary* to the hypothesis, there is no significant difference in return.	Traditional approaches which treat risk by restricting membership on the approved list, may make further risk adjustments unnecessary when forecasts are collected in quantitative terms and feedback correction is used.

Evaluation of Alternative Decision-Making Systems / 159

7	t	+	+2.05	5%	The assumption made in Chapter 1 about the improvement likely through SDM over qualitative systems is *supported* by the results.	Quantitative systems, given the observation that the assumptions used to generate the qualitative data do not tend to support the hypothesis, when combined with feedback systems outperform traditional qualitative systems.
8	t	0	.38	70%	Sharpe's inference about the similarity of diagonal and responsiveness returns is *supported* by this study.	Simpler responsiveness-based systems can be used, at least initially, without fear of foregoing additional returns available with more complex systems which include non-systematic risk adjustment as well.
9	t	0	−.34	72%	The hypothesis that the compositions of diagonal and responsiveness do not differ in terms of their closeness to optimal portfolios is *supported* by the evidence.	Further support for 8. Ex post, therefore, it should be no more difficult to justify individual holdings to trustors under one management system than the other.
10	z	0	−18.9	0%	Sharpe's observation of conformity is, *contrary* to the hypothesis, not supported by this analysis. In fact, α would have to be as low as 53 percent before the hypothesis would not be rejected.	Although not significantly different in terms of return 8 or nearness to optimality 9, diagonal and beta portfolios do have significantly different composition. Consequently, Sharpe's measure would appear to be an unreliable approach to compare portfolios.

Table 5.5. (continued)

Evaluation of Hypotheses

No	s	d	Value	Sig	Inference	Management Implications
11	t	+	−1.8	94.6%	Strongly *contrary* to the hypothesis, the inclusion of management feedback significantly (at 5.4 percent) lowers returns.	Feedback, when the underlying process is highly unstable—see Figure 5.1—, to a complex system can actually degrade results. Or, overly fine tuning can produce a dynamically unstable result. Traditional systems which do *not* systematically evaluate management's market forecasts appear to be justifiable.
12	t	+	+1.56	8%	The results *support* the hypothesis that variance correction in addition to level correction improves system performance.	Variance correction treats the analysts' ability to assess their own degree of uncertainty and is an important component of an MDS. Traditional managers might refer to this as the "quality" of the forecast.
13	t	+	−.73	76%	Level corrections to analyst's forecasts *contrary* to the hypothesis, do not improve returns.	Level correction, usually the first step in building feedback systems, does not appear to be effective by itself unless combined with variance correction. This would argue for taking both steps initially, or none at all.

14	t	+	+1.2	13%	The inclusion of skewness, in the form of a quadratic vs linear beta model, appears to be *supported*, although *not very strongly* by the data.	Analysts' forecasts include valuable non-linearities in forecasted market responsiveness. Economic justification may be found in considerations of leverage, economies of scale, etc.
15	t	+	.83	21%	Although the sign is in the right direction, the hypothesis is *not strongly supported* by the data.	Triangular distributions can be justified based on their role in variance correction (12) or quantification (7). but not on their ability to significantly improve returns due to the incorporation of skewness.
16	t	+	-1.2	88%	*Contrary* to the hypothesis, lowering the risk level resulted in an increase in return.	This is at first a startling contradiction. Several independent studies by the bank indicated that if securities for which analysts had a poor forecasting record, regardless of return, were eliminated, performance improved. Dropping the risk level accomplishes the same prescreening effect.
17	t	+	-.65	74%	*Contrary* to the hypothesis, lowering the risk level resulted in an increase in return.	The screening phenomena observed in 16 is also present, although not as significantly, when the risk level is dropped to 2.5 percent instead of 10 percent.

Table 5.5. (continued)

No	s	d	Value	Sig	Evaluation of Hypotheses — Inference	Management Implications
18	t	+	-.008	53%	*Contrary* to the hypothesis, lowering the risk level resulted in a very slight increase in return.	When the risk level is further reduced from 2.5 percent to .1 percent, there is no significant difference in returns. Screening at these levels would appear to be just offset by the reduction in return.
19	t	+	1.05	16%	Although *not strongly*, the hypothesis of declining returns with lower risk probabilities is *supported* by the data for single stock systems with analyst and management feedback.	Unfortunately, while this result is consistent with investment theory, it is inconsistent with the behavior of diagonal-variance systems under similar risk reduction. This implies an interaction between effective risk and the management system.
20	t	+	+.26	40%	The hypothesis is *not supported*; returns for single stock systems without feedback are unaffected by a risk probability reduction from 2.5 percent to .1 percent.	While this result is inconsistent with 19 for lower risk levels, it is consistent with the low level risk reduction for diagonal-variance systems which also failed to effect returns. For both systems, risk reduction for already low risk levels, has no impact on returns.

21	−	−.87	20%	Although the sign is in the right direction, the hypothesis is *not strongly supported* by the evidence.	A review of the portfolio decisions reveals only a few cases in which the bound was exceeded, probably accounting for the low significance level. When the bound was exceeded, it was never more than about 3 percent of the portfolio.
22	−	−1.17	13%	The hypothesis appears to be *supported*, although *not strongly* by the data.	This result is consistent with 21 and suggests that unless legal barriers exist, upper bounds should be flexible enough to permit securities which experience a relative price increase to be held in excess of rigid limits.
23	+	−.73	76%	*Contrary* to the hypothesis, feedback on analyst level and variance does not make a significant contribution to return.	After the benefits of screening from a low risk level, further improvements do not come from including analyst feedback, beyond the subjective feedback during the forecast collection process in SDM.
24	+	−1.13	85%	*Contrary* to the hypothesis, feedback on analyst and management forecasts does not improve performance. In fact, there is a significant deterioration at the 15 percent level.	This reinforces 23 and suggests a compounding of the negative effects of analyst and management feedback at low risk levels.

would have happened if various alternative systems had been used. It is possible, however, to compare the performance of systems tested in this study relative to each other and to market conditions. Figure 5.3 is a performance measurement graph very similar to the format employed by A. G. Becker in his *Retirement Funds Evaluation Service* [3]. The horizontal axis measures, as it does in the A.G. Becker graph, the ratio of the standard deviation of the portfolio to the standard deviation of the market index. Unlike A. G. Becker who uses the S&P 500, the market index in Figure 5.3 is the DOW. The horizontal axis is also used to measure the ratio of the number of times the portfolio had a negative return to the number of times the market return was negative. This relative risk measure is consistent with the loss function for the portfolio manager given in Figure 3.10. The vertical axis indicates portfolio return relative to the DOW's return.

In the body of the graph the standard deviation risk coordinate is the point adjacent to the hypothesis number and letter which identify the management system. The head of each arrow identifies the negative return risk coordinate. The single stock system in hypothesis 22a, for example, had a relative return of 1.04, relative standard deviation of 1.52 and relative negative return of .89. The capital market lines can be used, in the spirit of Sharpe's reward to variability performance measure given in Chapter 2, to separate portfolio performance into superior and inferior categories. Data above either of the capital market lines represents superior performance, while data below indicates poor performance. The "capital market line" for negative returns also reflects the non-linearity of this risk measure. It is interesting to observe that for the three highest relative returns, the judgment about the quality of pension fund management is dependent upon the risk measure selected. In general, one would expect the negative return risk to be less than standard deviation risk as relative returns rise, and greater when they fall. While this does appear to be valid in Figure 5.3, 8b as well as several results not shown are exceptions to this rule.

The Bank Administration Institute return for 22a of 5.7 percent would have placed this computer model managed fund at the top of the lowest quartile for 5–10 million dollar funds as measured by A. G. Becker over the period. Nevertheless this is still encouraging, considering that the fund was limited to T-Bills which averaged 5.35 percent and was charged 2 percent adverse market movement on each equity trade. The median non-equity component which included long-term bonds, private placements, etc. for the A. G. Becker measured funds was 11.17 percent. The

Figure 5.3. Performance Measurement

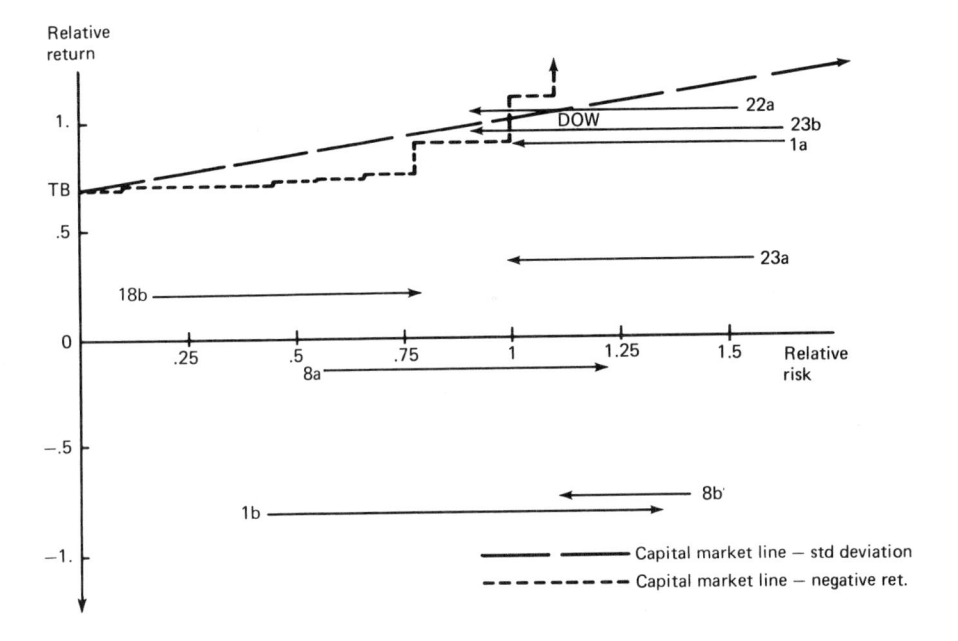

system performances shown in Figure 5.3 are representative of the phenomena that single stock, SDM type systems, the top three, outperformed portfolio, non-risk adjusted return qualitative or random systems. It is also apparent that systems without feedback correction tend to outperform those with it, e.g. 23b vs. 23a.

MANAGEMENT REPORTING SYSTEM

The mathematical style of presentation along with the complexity of various system alternatives could easily give the impression that any associated management reporting systems would be far too complicated to be used by pension fund managers. In the authors' experience the opposite has been true. In general, the more comprehensive and, therefore, usually more complex the inner workings of a Management Decision System, the simpler and more decision oriented can be the management reports. Conversely, systems which present data but which do not deal with the complexities of the problem simply pass these complexities along to the manager.

Monthly Reports—Security Analysis

To illustrate the form reports might take, a report module was added to the simulation program. Figures 5.4 and 5.5 illustrate for system 1b the management reports for periods 12 and 13. Current actions and resulting positions are given in terms of shares in the first three columns. T-Bills are stated as $100.00 securities to facilitate comparison with other holdings. Expectations are separated into certain dividends, expected price returns incorporating all probabilistic forecasts and feedback corrections, and the minimum returns consistent with the risk probability. Feedback coefficients are listed under the heading Forecast Adjustments. The level adjustment indicates the increase in return due to feedback correction. The level adjustment plus the ratio factor, times the current unadjusted forecast determines the corrected forecast. The last column is the ratio of the standard deviation of actual forecast errors to the forecasted standard deviation by the analyst.

If the analyst were a completely unbiased forecaster, the last three columns would contain 0, 1 and 1. From Figure 5.4, if we were in charge of Investment Research, we would see that a good portion of forecasted returns are due to level adjustments and not to the analysts' predictions.

Evaluation of Alternative Decision-Making Systems / **167**

Figure 5.4.

71/1 Stock	Actions Buy	Sell	Position Own	Expectations Dividend	Return	Minimum	Forecast Adjustments Level	Ratio	Deviation
AHC	10017	0	10017	242.10	11.588	2.608	6.950	0.362	1.183
AEP	15890	0	15890	2251.15	2.232	1.925	1.430	-0.055	1.108
AGRE	17067	0	17067	668.47	4.500	3.101	3.469	0.076	1.475
ABUD	12126	0	12126	505.28	1.933	1.606	1.400	-0.007	1.305
FDP	8533	0	8533	1194.72	3.327	2.064	2.217	0.329	1.226
GM	5689	0	5689	1611.92	3.367	1.802	2.910	0.132	1.932
S	6063	0	6063	682.13	2.982	1.759	2.301	0.123	1.066
SCE	14400	0	14400	1800.08	5.831	2.410	3.966	0.453	1.120
SPS	32915	0	32915	2029.80	4.844	4.502	3.935	0.008	1.421
SOH	5907	0	5907	1329.29	3.099	1.991	2.437	0.131	1.082
TXU	7554	0	7554	1133.16	2.506	2.367	1.808	0.038	1.258
VEL	19200	0	19200	1792.07	3.618	2.484	2.583	0.184	1.355
TBIL	37656	0	37656	14955.32	0.396	0.396			
Portfolio				$30195.46	2.576%				
					0.050%				

84.130 % Probability Monthly Return

Prior Month Recap
Return   0.304%
Selection Index   0.0 %
Current Market Value $9295491.00
Cash Generated   9437583.00
Net Cash Contribution   0.0
Management Fee Liability   78.33

168 / *A New Look at Portfolio Management*

Figure 5.5.

71/2 Stock	Actions Buy	Sell	Position Own	Expectations Dividend	Return	Minimum	Forecast Adjustments Level	Ratio	Deviation
AMC	190	0	10208	246.70	7.636	4.066	5.088	0.172	1.485
AEP	0	237	15652	2217.42	2.610	2.308	1.751	0.005	9.208
AGRE	0	1414	15652	613.05	5.356	1.534	4.738	0.062	15.372
ABUD	0	86	12040	501.68	2.016	1.534	1.545	-0.004	133.787
FDP	0	8533	0	0.0	4.271	-7.428	1.948	0.263	2.117
GM	0	5689	0	0.0	2.569	-1.755	2.104	0.125	13.498
NAL	22360	0	22360	745.35	7.475	1.668	6.269	0.233	8.637
S	0	193	5869	660.33	3.343	0.892	2.718	0.147	4.396
SCE	0	14400	0	0.0	7.221	-3.714	4.209	0.463	1.746
SPS	0	32915	0	0.0	5.750	-1.130	4.567	0.075	88.355
SDH	0	181	5726	1288.46	3.421	1.687	2.839	0.129	3.706
TET	11739	0	11739	1486.98	2.624	1.599	2.099	-0.097	1.097
TXU	19	0	7573	1136.06	2.249	1.748	1.666	0.008	20.504
VEL	364	0	19565	1826.11	2.804	1.769	1.814	0.060	3.115
TBIL	48026	0	48026	17044.67	0.354	0.354			
Portfolio				$27766.79	2.109%				
					0.306%				

84.130 % Probability Monthly Return

Prior Month Recap	
Return	0.920%
Selection Index	1.498%
Current Market Value	$9498379.00
Cash Generated	3795396.00
Net Cash Contribution	50000.00
Management Fee Liability	461.06

In the securities such as AGRE or SPS, the high values for level correction combined with the low ratio coefficients indicate that the analysts' predictions contribute only marginally to a forecast based on just a smoothed average of past returns. Negative ratio coefficients are indicative of turning point errors. If these negative coefficients were stable over time, i.e. the analyst was consistently always wrong, they would be just as valuable as if he were consistently right. Unfortunately, negative ratios tend to be small and vary in sign, as can be seen by referring to Figure 5.5, from period to period.

The Deviation ratios are all in excess of 1. Analysts, therefore, for the securities in the report, are effectively underestimating their conditional forecast uncertainty. The logical effect of supplying what portfolio managers call "poor quality" forecasts, can be seen by looking at ABUD on Figure 5.5. The underestimate of forecast error combined with a turning point mistake was sufficient to increase the downside risk enough to cause its sale.*

Monthly Reports—Portfolio Analysis

The summary line below the individual security data gives the overall dividend income for cash flow planning purposes and the expected price return for the portfolio. The next line shows, given the risk probability, the minimum expected return. These two summary lines provide the portfolio manager with the forecast data he needs to plan cash flows with the Trustor and to analyze tradeoffs between minimum return and downside risk exposure.

Monthly Reports—Performance Analysis

The Prior Month Recap section at the bottom of the monthly report shows the current status of the fund. The selection index is defined in (146) and for 71/1 shows that no securities were held in common with the perfect knowledge, optimal portfolio. Figure 5.6 presents the diversification summary for system 1b over the simulation period. In essence, for the first eleven months during which feedback coefficients were being de-

---

* The large value for the Deviation is not the direct result of an overly confident analyst, but due to the reduction in subjective variance because of the near zero value of the ratio correction. This can be seen by referring to (79). In future models, the variance of the correction factors could be included to make this a more appropriate management measure.

170 / *A New Look at Portfolio Management*

Figure 5.6.

1 TBIL								
1.000								
2 CDA	JOL	TBIL						
0.049	0.049	0.902						
3 JOL	MOT	TBIL						
0.049	0.049	0.902						
4 CWE	JOL	TBIL						
0.049	0.049	0.902						
5 CBM	CWE	FAC	ITT	LLY	MHP	TBIL		
0.049	0.048	0.049	0.049	0.049	0.049	0.706		
6 AGRE	TBIL							
0.049	0.0951							
7 AGRE	TBIL							
0.049	0.951							
8 TBIL								
1.000								
9 TBIL								
1.000								
10 TBIL								
1.000								
11 TBIL								
1.000								
12 AHC	AEP	AGRE	ABUD	FDP	GM	S	SCE	SPS	SOM	TXU	VEL	TBIL
0.050	0.050	0.050	0.050	0.050	0.050	0.050	0.050	0.050	0.050	0.050	0.050	0.405

Evaluation of Alternative Decision-Making Systems / **171**

13 AHC 0.049	AEP 0.049	AGRE 0.049	ABUD 0.049	NAL 0.049	S 0.049	SOH 0.049	TET 0.049	TXU 0.049	VEL 0.049	TBIL 0.506	
14 ABC 0.049	AGRE 0.049	MO 0.049	S 0.048	TET 0.049	TBIL 0.756						
15 AGHE 0.049	CSR 0.049	FJO 0.049	GMT 0.049	GE 0.049	MA 0.049	MO 0.049	SRL 0.049	S 0.049	WIN 0.049	TBIL 0.506	
16 AGRE 0.049	GE 0.049	HJ 0.049	INA 0.049	MA 0.049	SRL 0.049	TET 0.049	WIN 0.049	TBIL 0.605			
17 ABC 0.049	FDS 0.049	TBIL 0.902									
18 AGRE 0.050	BHW 0.050	CLX 0.050	FJO 0.050	HIA 0.050	IFF 0.050	JNJ 0.050	KG 0.050	PABT 0.050	SYN 0.050	XRX 0.050	TBIL 0.455
19 AGI 0.049	CLX 0.049	FJO 0.049	HIA 0.049	JNJ 0.049	PABT 0.049	XRX 0.049	TBIL 0.655				
20 CLX 0.049	XDOW 0.951										
21 CLX 0.050	MNC 0.050	TBIL 0.900									
22 TBIL 1.000											

veloped, but not used, the analysts' uncertainty was sufficient, given the risk probability of 15.87 percent, to keep the fund out of the equity markets. When feedback correction was introduced in period 12, the very low Ratio corrections sufficiently reduced the estimated variance and combined with a market recovery to cause the portfolio to reenter the equity markets. As the feedback factors were updated and the market began its decline in period 16, the Deviation correction offset the Ratio correction effect and the portfolio again retreated into T-Bills and the DOW.

System Design

The entire test system is designed in a modular structure. There is a separate command for each objective function, the market model estimation, feedback correction, the revision algorithm and management reports.

Modules have been written in a computer independent version of FORTRAN and share common data structures. This approach follows the author's Investment Analysis Language [5] and, in fact, permits the entire IAL system to be used in conjunction with the systems in this study. The advantage, of course, is that IAL programs to forecast price distributions as a function of company characteristics, such as earnings per share growth, earnings instability, etc. can be easily incorporated into portfolio management systems. In this vein, the portfolio mangement systems discussed in this study could be constructed to select among alternative forecasters or models for the same investment as well as to select alternative investments.

The modular, FORTRAN structure should permit, as it has for IAL bank planning systems, integration with operational pension data processing systems written in COBOL.

Operating costs are difficult to estimate from the simulation. On the one hand, the simulation performs many calculations which would not be done in an operational system. Conversely, the data controls in the simulation are not adequate for a commercial application. Nevertheless, on the assumption that these two aspects approximately offset each other, the average cost at prime time commercial 360–65 rates charged by Cornell University in 1974 was on the order of one tenth of a cent per security in the approved universe per decision period. This estimate assumes a 234 security universe and would decline exponentially for smaller approved lists. It is also based on a sample of the most complex systems employing full feedback correction facilities and hard upper bounds.

SUMMARY

In this chapter twenty-four specific hypotheses about the structure of pension fund management systems are formulated and tested. The conclusions differ in many respects from current theoretical views and in general support a number, but not all, of the approaches traditionally taken by portfolio managers. For example, the following conclusions selected from Table 5.5 are directly counter to current academic criticism of professional portfolio management.

1. Traditional, one stock at a time management systems may be superior to normative portfolio management schemes proposed by the academic community.
2. Market efficiency, transaction costs and fees do not seem to preclude better than randomly generated returns. Thus it would appear that pension fund (or portfolio managers in general) can legitimately refute the dart board characterization placed upon them.
3. Feedback, when the underlying process is highly unstable (see Figure 5.1) to a complex system can actually degrade results. Or, overly fine tuning can produce a dynamically unstable result. Traditional systems which do *not* systematically evaluate management's market forecasts appear to be justifiable.
4. Lowering the risk level resulted in an increase in return. This is at first a startling contradicition [to investment theory]. Several independent studies by the bank indicated that if securities for which analysts had a poor forecasting record, regardless of return, were eliminated, performance improved. Dropping the risk level accomplishes the same prescreening effect. On the other hand, certain traditional portfolio management approaches were shown to reduce performance. Again, from Table 5.5:

1. Quantitative systems, given the observation that the assumptions used to generate the qualitative data do not tend to support the hypothesis (that quantitative systems are superior to qualitative), when combined with feedback systems outperform traditional qualitative systems.
2. Unless legal barriers exist, upper bounds should be flexible enough to permit securities which experience a relative price increase to be held in excess of rigid limits.

These conclusions are reinforced by the scope of the forecast data and the institutional detail considered in the management simulations. At a minimum, the results encourage a reexamination of the relevance of macro capital asset pricing concepts to the decision-making of market participants at the micro level. When the risks of falling below the downside return estimate are in the 10 percent and below range, portfolio performance is comparable to the performance obtained by pension fund managers during the same period. Thus the goal of achieving comparable results with mathematical models appears to have been met. The form of risk measurement is also shown to have a critical effect on the judgment of performance quality. The associated computer systems are modularly constructed, integratable into daily operations and operate at very low cost.

Chapter 6

Conclusion

SUMMARY OF MAJOR FINDINGS

Even though the scope of this dissertation is limited in Chapter 1, the results contain implications for a wide spectrum of portfolio managers, security analysts and management scientists. Perhaps the best way to review the major findings of this research is to consider the direct implications for each of these professional groups.

Portfolio Management

Several conclusions can clearly be drawn from this investigation and experimental results.

1. Flow charting the behavioral management process is an important step prior to making changes through the incorporation of new management technology.

2. Portfolio management, even after many simplifying assumptions, is a highly complex, but inherently mathematical process.

3. Traditional qualitative management systems do not perform as well as quantitative approaches and make system analysis and improvement virtually impossible.

4. Traditional, one stock at a time, portfolio management with an emphasis on Prudent Man downside risk yields as much perfor-

mance, if not more, than newer portfolio management techniques based on beta models.

5. Built-in forecast quality controls and automatically corrective feedback do not insure an improvement in performance. Sophisticated feedback, due to underlying instability in forecast errors, may actually hurt performance. However, it is possible that even though simple level and ratio adjustment is not effective, more complex systems which include the uncertainty in the feedback coefficients might be effective. The significant improvement caused by variance or forecast quality correction is an indication of this potential.

6. The difference between measuring risk according to Prudent Man norms vs portfolio theory can make all the difference in evaluating the quality of portfolio management.

7. Interactions between the nature of the management system and the form of portfolio objectives make forecasting the likely impact of perceived risk reduction very difficult. The conflicting effects of screening vs declining economic return dictate at least some type of simulation study for each specific case.

8. Much of the risk amenable to quantitative control may be already taken out in the process of constructing the approved list. This would suggest, if legally feasible, dealing with much larger approved lists to permit substantive risk-return analyses.

9. Soft upper bounds improve performance and do not appear to lead to undue concentrations. This is in contrast to Senate proposals which would have imposed a 5 percent tax on holdings in excess of 5 percent [17].

10. The portfolio management tools developed in Chapter 4 can be introduced one step at a time and at very low technical cost. The impact on personnel, however, can be severe and, in the author's experience, needs to be mollified by extensive educational programs.

11. Given the same underlying forecasts supplied by security analysts, changes in the portfolio management system or in management parameters can have a substantial impact on performance. In short, bad performance can just as easily be the result of an inappropriate management system as it can be the result of poor security analysis.

Security Analysts

The focus of this study is on portfolio management and not security analysis. However, significant implications can still be drawn.

1. Security analysts can make forecasts which permit attainment of significantly better than random returns after all management fees and transaction costs are included.
2. Quantitative systems based on triangular distributions are a practical way to collect price forecasts and clearly improve performance over unconditional qualitative recommendations.
3. Feedback correction, based on an analysis of past errors, is of questionable value due to the instability of forecast errors.
4. If subjective beta models are employed, they should include a quadratic as well as a linear term.

Management Scientists

A number of suggestions are made and implied throughout this study toward the solution of problems encountered in the implementation of management science concepts. Several overall observations summarizing these suggestions are presented below.

1. Traditional portfolio management practices, while seemingly inefficient on the surface, may not be too far from the best, robust approach to the problem.
2. Institutional considerations may make general normative approaches inappropriate, needlessly complex and above all, ineffective.
3. A behavioral framework is a necessary, but not sufficient, condition to enable management science activities to produce real organizational change.

In this section we have reviewed the major findings and direct implications for three professional disciplines. In the remaining two sections broader implications for research and portfolio management strategies are examined.

FUTURE RESEARCH

Extensions

There are a number of important areas of portfolio management that are direct extensions of this study and merit further research. Several such areas and associated ramifications are outlined below.

1. Can analysts forecast time patterns of conditional price movements that contain significantly more information than the future spot forecasts made in SDM? If they can, only then are multi-period extensions of the revision algorithm justified.

2. Would the inclusion of the variance effects due to feedback coefficient instability change the negative conclusion about the performance value of automatic feedback correction? If the answer is affirmative, only then should the additional complexities and costs incurred by instituting feedback systems be addressed.

3. Can the results presented in this study be replicated for other pension fund management institutions over the same and more recent time periods? This question is critical, if the conclusions reached are to be used beyond the bank that supplied the data for this study.

4. Do beta models, either linear or quadratic, estimated from past data generate necessarily lower performance than that obtained with analysts' forecasts? If this hypothesis can be rejected, then, at a minimum, analysts' efforts would be redirected toward those securities for which they had a comparative forecasting advantage.

5. Do fundamental models, e.g. those by Gordon [41], Nerlove [57] or the author [4], when augmented by market factors provide a better way than beta models for analysts to translate their corporate forecasts into price forecasts? If this is true, then a resurgence in fundamental research can be justified.

6. Are alternative distributions, e.g. beta, more effective than triangular distributions in collecting subjective data? Or, would collecting the interquartile range and the most likely be more effective than the low, most likely, high approach? As a further extension, might some form of Bayesian revision for future spot forecasts be justified.?

The questions listed above are well defined, empirical issues concerning pension fund management that can only be resolved by further testing with *ex-anti* as well as *ex post* market data. The results in this study, however, also raise general theoretical concerns. For example, the general tendency for almost all feedback models to degenerate to a positive level and a very small ratio coefficient would strongly indicate that *ex post* results are not on average equal to *ex-anti* expectations over the decision-making cycle. This last qualification is important, for even though one would expect equality in the long run, in the short run it may never be true. Unfortunately, tests of capital asset pricing hypotheses almost always assume equality regardless of the return horizon. It would seem, from the results in this study, that this assumption is of questionable validity. Further conflicts between the results in this study and capital asset equilibrium assumptions can be found in such areas as the difference between downside probability risk required by Prudent Man law and quadratic utility or the widely observed one stock at a time decision-making behavior and portfolio balancing.

MANAGEMENT STRATEGY

Many of the marketing issues facing executives in portfolio management have already been discussed in Chapter 2. Recently, Bankers Trust Company published a study titled *The Private Pension Controversy* [15], which covers a wide range of legislative proposals for pension reform and control. Whatever develops, either in the marketplace or in Congress, it is clear that investment decisions by portfolio managers are coming and will continue to come under increasing public scrutiny. In a March 9, 1974 issue of *Business Week*, an article with the title "Telling more at Citibank" which lists major portfolio decisions made by First National City Bank during 1973, is dramatic evidence of this trend. As the rate of disclosure has increased, so has the volatility of stock and bond prices. Banks could conceivably find themselves disclosing potentially embarrassing rapid reversals of policy. In fact, the article cited from *Business Week* states:

> In the same way, IBM was both a major buy and a major sell. This raises the question of whether Citibank succeeded in buying low and selling high (or vice versa), but Heilshorn says this was not necessarily the case. "It was a question," he says, "of adjusting new clients' portfolios to the portfolio proportions we recommended.

In short, all firms managing pension funds are now required under the

1974 pension reform legislation to justify their decision-making process.*
Heilshorn could also have been asked whether Citibank sold IBM from one large, important account and bought it in a number of smaller, less influential accounts at the same time. Without strong, tangible support that the risk-return goals of each account warranted such action, Citibank would have a hard time defending this or similar decisions even though they might have been in the best interests of all concerned. Even in cases where normal forecasting errors were made, pressures are bound to be brought to bear to prove that the error could not have been reduced. The new pension law provides an added incentive by making "fiduciaries liable for any loss to the plan occurring because the fiduciary standards were disregarded." The data collected through structured decision-making systems of the type presented in this study can provide the strong, tangible support needed to justify portfolio decisions. Indeed the rational structure and use of such systems can be important assets in themselves in the defense of decision quality. Beyond helping executive management to cope with the pressures raised by disclosure, structured decision-making systems can play an important role in other aspects of management strategy formulation.

The ability to change explicitly and quickly both the form of portfolio goals and risk-return parameters is a valuable capability in light of the uncertainty surrounding future federal or state fiduciary standards.

Although feedback systems applied mechanically do not improve performance, they do provide very useful evaluations of analysts' forecasting abilities. The experimental results in this study do not rule out benefits from using these evaluations as the basis for salary incentives to encourage analysts to improve their security analysis methods.

The low cost of the revision algorithm could foster new fiduciary services. The distinction between dividend and price return makes the introduction of ordinary and capital gains taxation a straightforward extension. This ability combined with low cost, explicit risk-return tradeoffs and diversification controls could be the foundation for personal money management services in retail banking and brokerage.

Finally, a study of alternative investments to U.S. equities and Treasury Bills by Robichek, Cohn and Pringle [59] concluded:

---

*See HR2(PL93-406) - The Employee Retirement Income Security Act passed in 1974.

The large number of negative or insignificantly positive correlation coefficients leads to the conclusion that diversification among the twelve investment media may lead to improved portfolio efficiency in the mean-standard deviation context.

Given this evidence, if the approved list were intended to include investments beyond U.S. equities and Treasury Bills, it is possible that the performance reported in Chapter 5 would be significantly improved.

The general structure of the portfolio management systems developed in Chapter 4 makes it very easy to add new investment forms. Bonds, for example, could be included by asking analysts to forecast yield curves for acceptable ratings and then, by using the bond pricing commands in the IAL System [5], converting these yield curves into expected, conditional returns. Given the recent equity market volatility and the generally high yields of long term bonds, it is very likely that the revision algorithm developed in this book, when set to minimize downside exposure, would transfer a large percentage from equities to bonds. The magnitude of this shift, however, would not be the same for all accounts, but individually taylored to account goals, and management abilities. Without the systems developed in Chapter 4, however, it would be difficult at best to make the management decision to expand the approved list and almost impossible to justify this decision to clients and to regulators if the results were not successful.

The purpose of this study given in the Preface is to promote better management of pension funds by institutional investors and to provide tools to aid them in improving their management processes. Although the experimental results raise at least as many questions as they answer, the author hopes that the results and ideas contained in this study are a firm and constructive step toward better portfolio management.

BIBLIOGRAPHY

1. Ackoff, R. L. "Management Misinformation Systems," *Management Science*, December 1967.
2. A. G. Becker and Co. *Annual Report 1971*, Chicago, 1972.
3. A. G. Becker and Co. *Retirement Funds Evaluation Service*, Chicago, 1972.
4. Ahlers, D. M. "SEM: A Security Evaluation Model," Chap. 13 in Cohen, K. J. and Hammer, F. S. (eds.) *Analytical Methods in Banking*, Homewood, Illinois: Irwin, 1966; and Chap. 11 in Elton, E. J. and Gruber, M. J. (eds.) *Security Evaluation and Portfolio Analysis*, Englewood Cliffs: Prentice-Hall, 1972.
5. Ahlers, D. M. *Investment Analysis Language Manual*, American Bankers Association, Washington, D.C., 1970.
6. Ahlers, D. M. "SDM: A Structured Decision Making System for Portfolio Management," *Proceedings of the Institute of Quantitative Research*, New York, April 1970.
7. Ahlers, D. M. and Martin, A. "The Investment Manager's Information System: Computerized Approaches to Portfolio and Performance Analysis," Speech, ABA Trust Conference, New Orleans, March 1972.
8. Ahlers, D. M. and Steglitz, M. H. "The Use and Misuse of Security Evaluation Models," *Proceedings of the University of Chicago Seminar on the Analysis of Security Prices*, Chicago: Graduate School of Business, May 1968.
9. Ahlers, D. M. and Steglitz, M. H. "The Effect of Institutional Arrangements for Decision Making on the Selection of Portfolios," *Proceedings of the University of Chicago Seminar on the Analysis of Security Prices*, Chicago: Graduate School of Business, November 1968.
10. American Institute of Banking. *Trust Department Services*, Washington, D.C., 1954.
11. Argyris, C. "Management Information Systems: The Challenge to Rationality and Emotionality," *Management Science*, Vol. 17, No. 6, February 1971, pp. 275–292.
12. Bank Administration Institute. *Measuring the Investment Performance of Pension Funds*, Park Ridge, Illinois, 1968.
13. Bank Aministration Institute. *Supplement to Measuring the Investment Performance of Pension Funds—Risk and the Evaluation of Pension Fund Performance*, Park Ridge, Illinois, 1968.
14. Bankers Trust Company. *Bankers Trust 1972 Study of Employee Savings and Thrift Plans*, New York, 1972.
15. Bankers Trust Company. *The Private Pension Controversy*, New York, 1973.
16. Baumol, W. J. "An Expected Gain Confidence Limit Criterion for Portfolio Selection," *Management Science*, Vol. 10, No. 1, October 1963, pp. 174–182.
17. Belair, F. "Pension-Fund Curb Is Opposed," *The New York Times*, February 6, 1974, p. 45.
18. Belleveau, N. "Discretion or indiscretion? It's just possible a manager can be sued even if the endowment is up," *Institutional Investor*, August 1972, p. 65.

Conclusion / **183**

19. Bonini, Charles P. *Simulation of Information and Decision Systems in the Firm,* Englewood Cliffs: Prentice-Hall, 1963.
20. Brown, R. G. *Smoothing, Forecasting and Prediction of Discrete Time Series,* Englewood Cliffs: Prentice-Hall, 1963.
21. Cantor, R. "Why Banks Have Trouble Managing Investment Accounts," *Institutional Investor,* Vol. 2, No. 9, New York, September 1968.
22. Chapman, L. J. and Chapman, J. P. "Genesis of Popular but Erroneous Psychodiagonstic Observations," *Journal of Abnormal Psychology,* Vol. 72, 1967, pp. 193–204.
23. Chen, A., Jen, F. and Zionts, S. "The Optimal Portfolio Revision Policy," *Journal of Business,* Vol. 44, No. 1, January 1971.
24. Clarkson, G. P. E. *Portfolio Selection: A Simulation of Trust Investment,* Englewood Cliffs: Prentice-Hall, 1962.
25. Cohen, K. J. and Pogue, J. A. "An Empirical Evaluation of Alternative Portfolio-Selection Models," *Journal of Business,* Vol. 40, No. 1, April 1967, pp. 166–193.
26. Comptroller of the Currency. *Fiduciary Powers of National Banks and Collective Investment Funds Regulation 9,* Washington, D.C.: U.S. Government Printing Office, 1964.
27. Cyert, R. M. and March, J. G. *A Behavioral Theory of the Firm,* Englewood Cliffs: Prentice-Hall, 1963.
28. Ehrlich, E. C. "The Functions and Investment Policies of Personal Trust Departments," *Monthly Review of the Federal Reserve Bank of New York,* October 1972, pp. 255–270; and continued in January 1973, pp. 12–19.
29. Elton, E. J. and Gruber, M. J. (eds.) *Security Evaluation and Portfolio Analysis,* Englewood Cliffs: Prentice-Hall, 1972.
30. Fama, E. F. "Risk, Return and Equilibrium: Some Clarifying Comments," *Journal of Finance,* Vol. 23, No. 1, March 1968, pp. 29–40.
31. Farnum, C. W. "Corporate Fiduciaries of Employee Benefit Funds—An Outline of Responsibilities and Supervision," *Old Age Income Assurance, Part V,* Washington, D.C.: Joint Economic Committee, Congress of the United States, U.S. Government Printing Office, 1968, pp. 257–263.
32. Farnum, C. W., private correspondence.
33. Feigenbaum, E. and Feldman, J. *Computers and Thought,* New York: McGraw-Hill, 1963.
34. Feldman, J. "Simulation of Behavior in the Binary Choice Experiment," in Feignebaum, E. and Feldman, J. (eds.) *Computers and Thought,* New York: McGraw-Hill, 1963.
35. *Financial Executive,* February 1972, p. 14.
36. Fiske, H. S. "Fidelity: The problems of success," *The Institutional Investor,* Vol. 3, No. 3, New York, 1969.
37. Freund, J. E. *Mathematical Statistics,* Englewood Cliffs: Prentice-Hall, 1962.
38. Friend, I. and Blume, M. "Measurement of Portfolio Performance Under Uncertainty," *American Economic Review,* September 1970, pp. 561–575.

39. Glauber, R. *Appendix to Herrick Management and Research Company,* Cambridge: Harvard Business School, 1971.
40. Goldberg, L. R. "Simple Models or Simple Processes? Some Research on Clinical Judgments," *American Psychologist,* Vol. 23, 1968, pp. 483–496.
41. Gordon, M. J. "The Savings, Investment and Valuation of a Corporation," *Review of Economics and Statistics,* Vol. 44, February 1962, pp. 37–51.
42. Hicks, E. L. *Accounting For The Cost Of Pension Plans—Accounting Research Study No. 8,* New York: American Institute of Certified Public Accounts, Inc., 1965.
43. International Business Machines, Inc. *IBM Portfolio Selection Program (IBPS 90),* New York, 1962.
44. Jensen, M. "The Performance of Mutual Funds in the Period 1945–1964," *Journal of Finance,* Vol. 42, April 1969, pp. 167–247.
45. Klemkosky, R. C. "The Bias In Composite Performance Measures," *Journal of Financial and Quantitative Analysis,* Seattle: University of Washington Graduate School of Business Administration, June 1973, pp. 505–512.
46. Leavitt, H. J. "Applied Organization Change In Industry: Structural, Technical, and Human Approaches," Chap. 4 in Cooper, W. W., *et al.* (eds.) *New Perspectives In Organization Research,* New York: Wiley, 1964.
47. Levy, R. A. "Stationarity of Beta Coefficients," *Financial Analysts Journal,* November-December 1971, pp. 55–69.
48. Lintner, J. "Security Prices, Risk and Maximal Gains from Diversification," *Journal of Finance,* December 1965, pp. 587–615.
49. Malkiel, B. G. "Equity Yields, Growth and the Structure of Share Prices," *American Economic Review,* Vol. 53, No. 5, December 1963, pp. 1004–1031.
50. Markowitz, H. "Portfolio Selection," *Journal of Finance,* March 1952, pp. 77–91.
51. Markowitz, H. "The Optimization of a Quadratic Function Subject to Linear Constraints," *Naval Research Logistics Quarterly,* March–June 1956, pp. 111–133.
52. Markowitz, H. *Portfolio Selection: Efficient Diversification of Investments,* New York: Wiley, 1959.
53. Michaels, C. *Profile of the security analyst, 1969,* New York: don Howard-Personnel Inc., 1969.
54. Miller, F. A. "The Magical Number Seven Plus or Minus Two: Some Limits on Our Capability for Processing Information," *Psychological Review,* 1956, pp. 81–97.
55. Mlynarczyk, F. "Alpha, Beta, Omega," *Institutional Investor,* New York, July 1972.
56. Moody's Investors Services, Inc. *Moody's Dividend Record,* Vols. 40, 41 and 42, New York.
57. Nerlove, M. "Factors Affecting Differences Among Rates of Return on Investments in Individual Common Stocks," *Review of Economics and Statistics,* Vol. 50, No. 3, August 1968, pp. 312–331.

58. Pogue, G. "An Intertemporal Model for Investment Management," *Journal of Bank Research,* Spring 1970.
59. Robichek, A., Cohn, R. and Pringle, J. "Returns on Alternative Investment Media and Implications for Portfolio Construction," *Journal of Business,* Vol. 45, No. 3, July 1972, pp. 427–443.
60. Sharpe, W. F. "A Simplified Model for Portfolio Analysis," *Management Science,* January 1963, pp. 277–293.
61. Sharpe, W. F. "Capital Asset Prices: A Theory of Market Equilibrium Under Conditions of Risk," *Journal of Finance,* September 1964, pp. 425–442.
62. Sharpe, W. F. "Mutual Fund Performance," *Journal of Business: A Supplement,* No. 1, Part 2, January 1966, pp. 119–138.
63. Sharpe, W. F. *Portfolio Theory and Capital Markets,* New York: McGraw-Hill, 1970.
64. Shelly, II, M. W. and Bryan, G. L. (eds.) *Human Judgements and Optimality,* New York: Wiley, 1964.
65. Siegel, S. *Nonparametric Statistics,* New York: McGraw-Hill, 1956.
66. Simon, H. A. *Administrative Behavior,* Seventh Printing, New York: Macmillan, 1953.
67. Simon, H. A. "On the Concept of Organizational Goal," *Administrative Science Quarterly,* No. 9, June 1964, pp. 1–22.
68. Skinner, B. F. "Superstition in the Pigeon," *Journal of Experimental Psychology,* Vol. 38, 1948, pp. 168–172.
69. Slovic, P. "Psychological Study of Human Judgement: Implications for Investment Decision Making," *Journal of Finance,* Vol. 27, No. 4, September 1972, pp. 779–799.
70. Smidt, S. and Brenner, M. "Predicting Changes in Systematic Risk: Theory and Evidence," unpublished *Cornell Working Paper,* 1974.
71. Smith, J. L *Mathematical Aspects of Investment Decision-Making With Application to the Stock Market,* unpublished Ph.D. Dissertation, UCLA, 1971.
72. Smith, K. *Portfolio Mangement,* New York: Holt, Rinehart and Winston, 1971.
73. Stone, B. and Reback, R. "Linear Programming Models for Managing Portfolio Revisons," *Journal of Bank Research,* forthcoming.
74. Theil, H. *Applied Economic Forecasting,* North-Holland, Amsterdam, 1966.
75. Treynor, J. L. and Mazuy, K. K. "Can Mutual Funds Outguess the Market?," *Harvard Business Review,* Vol. 44, No. 4, July–August 1966, pp. 131–136.
76. Turing, A. M. "Computing Machinery and Intelligence," *Mind,* Vol. 59, October 1950, pp. 433–460.
77. Van Horn, R. L. "Validation of Simulation Results," *Management Science,* Vol. 17, No. 5, January 1971, pp. 247–258.
78. Williams, J. B. *The Theory of Investment Value,* Cambridge, 1938.
79. Williamson, J. P. *Investments: New Analytic Techniques,* New York: Praeger, 1971.

80. Winer, B. J. *Statistical Principles In Experimental Design*, New York: McGraw-Hill, 1962.
81. Winkler, Robert L. "The Consensus of Subjective Probability Distributions," *Management Science*, Vol. 15, No. 2, October 1968, pp. 61–75.

APPENDIX A

SECURITY UNIVERSE

188 / *A New Look at Portfolio Management*

Ticker Symbols for Securities in Sample

ACF	ARC	CBM	DAL	GE	IK	MA	MO	SCE	R
AMF	AVP	C	DOV	GIS	IP	MYG	P	SO	UAL
AMP	BAMR	CS	DOW	GM	ITT	MHP	PBI	SGA	UMM
ARA	BAX	CSGA	DOWJ	GTE	JWC	MRK	PCO	SPS	USG
ABT	BDX	CLX	DUK	GP	JM	MSU	PRD	SY	UT
AIN	BHW	CGP	DNB	GS	JNJ	MMM	PTN	SQB	UPJ
ACD	BNL	KO	DD	GR	JOL	MOB	PG	SN	VEL
AA	BDK	CL	EFU	GT	K	MTC	OAT	SOH	WB
AHC	BA	CK	EK	GEI	KDE	MCL	RCA	STY	HIR
AMR	BCC	CBS	EMR	GTY	KMB	MOT	RAL	STN	WLA
ABC	BN	CWE	FAC	GNN	KG	NLTC	RTN	SWX	WBC
ACY	BMY	CQ	FJQ	GO	LOF	NAL	REV	SYN	WU
AEP	BHS	CFD	FDS	GTU	LLY	NCR	RJR	TBIL	W
ASP	BC	CNG	FLD	HNZ	LNL	DR	RXM	TRW	WY
AGI	BUR	CAL	FIR	HIA	LTR	NIEL	RD	TE	WHR
AGRE	BGH	CIC	FBKS	HON	LLX	NWA	SA	TPAX	WIN
AHP	CCB	CIL	FNB	HFC	LST	NOB	SIPL	TX	Z
AHS	CMK	CTC	FNC	HOU	MZ	OT	SRT	TET	XRX
AST	CPL	CDA	FLG	HJ	MAG	OCF	SGP	TXU	ZAL
T	CRR	GLW	FDP	INA	MRO	PPG	SPP	TU	ZE
TW	CAT	CCK	FPL	IPC	M	PABT	SRL	TWA	
ABUD	CZ	ZB	F	IBM	MHS	JCP	S	TA	
ACK	CSR	DLP	GMT	IFF	MNC	PEP	SVM	UCC	
DG	CMB	DE				PFE	SMF	UK	

APPENDIX B

SYMBOL GLOSSARY

The following table contains definitions of symbols used beyond the page on which they are first introduced or the following page. This limitation is employed to avoid unnecessarily lengthening the glossary to include variables defined only to simplify intermediate substitutions.

Symbol	Represents	Superscripts and subscripts	Defined (page)	Units
α	feedback correction smoothing parameter		83	—
α_i	intercept in subjective β model-non-systematic return	security in universe	91	%/period
α_s	intercept in ex post estimated β model-non-systematic return	single stock vs portfolio	20	%/period
a	intercept in feedback correction model	sub-indicates variables being corrected, i.e. i-security M-Index Q-Index^2	93	%/period

190 / A New Look at Portfolio Management

Symbol	Represents	Superscripts and subscripts	Defined (page)	Units
β_i	market coefficient responsiveness in subjective β model	security in universe	91	—
β_p	market coefficient in ex post β model systematic return	portfolio vs. single stock	20	—
β_s	market coefficient in ex post β model systematic return	single stock vs portfolio sub- i indicates security	20	—
b	slope in feedback correction model	sub-see "a"	93	—
$_iD$	forecasted dividend	security in universe	103	\$/mth
D_I	forecasted dividend	DOW index	81	\$/mth
e	error in forecast equation		20	%/period
E( )	expectation operator- also indicated by a "–" over the variable		20	—
f_i	management fee	sub- 1, –, N–2 securities N–1 market fund N 30 Day T-Bills	103	%/mth
h_i	current holdings forecast for conditional DOW	see "f_i"	102	% portfolio
$\bar{I}_j$	level in environment j	sub- j 1 of 3 mutually exclusive environments; H-Highest expected in j L-Lowest expected in j	80	\$

Appendix B: Symbol Glossary / **191**

Symbol	Represents	Superscripts and subscripts	Defined (page)	Units
J	length of moving average consistent with feedback smoothing	see "α"	83	months
K	downside risk parameter-number of standard deviations below estimated mean portfolio return		107	—
K_i^β	security return, feedback corrected and adjusted by its contribution to β risk for the portfolio.	see "f_i"	119	%/mth
K_i^N	randomly generated inputs for the revision algorithm	see "f_i"	128	0/1
K_i^Q	expected security return, feedback corrected, translated into qualitative buy, hold and sell inputs	see "f_i"	127	0/1/–1
K_i^ρ	expected security return feedback corrected and downside risk adjusted on a stock by stock vs portfolio basis	see "f_i"	124	%/mth
K_i^R	expected security return, feedback corrected but with no risk adjustment	see "f_i"	126	%/mth
K_i^Y	expected security return, feedback corrected and adjusted by its contribution to portfolio downside risk	see "f_i"	110	%/mth

Symbol	Represents	Superscripts and subscripts	Defined (page)	Units
$\tilde{m}_j$	conditional forecasted price return in excess of T-Bill return for the DOW Index	see "$\bar{I}_j$"	81	%/mth
M_j	conditional expected price return in excess of T-Bill return for the DOW Index	see "$\bar{I}_j$"	82	%/mth
M	unconditional expected price return in excess of T-Bill return for the DOW Index	see "$\bar{I}_j$" sup-c-feedback corrected	82	%/mth
N	total number of securities, equities, market fund and T-Bills		101	—
$\tilde{P}_i$	conditional security price level in environment j	sub-j 1 of 3 mutually exclusive environments H-highest forecasted in j. M-most likely forecasted in j. L-lowest forecasted in j.	85	$
$_iP$	unconditional expected security price	sub-see f_i sub-c-feedback corrected	114	$
p_j	probability of environment j	see "$\bar{I}_j$"	80	—
ρ	probability of falling below a given portfolio return-downside risk parameter		108	—

Appendix B: Symbol Glossary / 193

Symbol	Represents	Superscripts and subscripts	Defined (page)	Units
Q_j	conditional, expected, squared excess DOW price return	see "$\tilde{I}_j$"	84	$\%^2$/mth
Q	unconditional, expected squared excess DOW price return	sup-c-feedback corrected	85	$\%^2$/mth
$\tilde{r}_j$	conditional, yearly excess security price return	see "$\tilde{I}_j$"	86	%/year
R_f	risk free monthly return, i.e. 90 day T-Bills 30 days prior to maturity stated on a dividend equivalent return basis		20	%/mth
R_m	expected market (DOW) return		20	%/mth
R_p	expected monthly portfolio return inclusive of all transaction costs and fees		20	%/mth
R_s	expected security market return		20	%/mth
$_iR$	unconditional, expected, excess price return	sub-i- see "f_i" sup-c-feedback corrected	91	%/mth
$_pR_j$	unconditional, expected return	sub-i- security price below which actual security price return should fall no more than p% of the time	123	

194 / *A New Look at Portfolio Management*

Symbol	Represents	Superscripts and subscripts	Defined (page)	Units
R_j	conditional expected monthly excess security price return	see "$\bar{I}_j$"	86	%/mth
σ	standard deviation	sub-indicates variable sup-2-variance c-feedback corrected	21	
s_i^2	unconditional, expected security return variance including feedback correction	see "a"	99	%²/mth
t_i	transaction cost for the ith security		102	%
u_i	maximum percent of portfolio in the ith security		106	%
V	factor to adjust yearly forecast variance to monthly variance		83	—
w_i	percent of portfolio in security i after revision	see "f_i"	101	%
z_i	percent of portfolio sold or bought in security i	see "f_i"	101	%

Index

A
Application problems
  management age, 17
  inappropriate theory, 44
  computer costs, 78
  See also Behavioral Flow analysis

B
Bank of New York, 26–28
Bankers Trust Company, 26–28
Baumol, W.J.
  gain confidence criteria, 45
Becker, A.G.
  performance evaluation study
    results, 19, 63, 164
Behavioral flow analysis
  contolled by security analysts, 33
  controlled by portfolio
    managers, 42
  of new structured Decision
    Making System, 52–53
Beta models
  performance measurement
    foundation, 20–21
  Sharpe computational
    assumptions, 50
  estimation of, 89–92
  feedback correction to, 97
  use in return estimation, 103
  absolute value correction of, 118
  performance of, 159
  See also Performance
    measurement, Sharpe,
    Computer codes

C
Capital Asset Pricing Model
  introudction to, 20–22
  See Beta models
Capital Market Line
  prudent man correction,
    164–165
Cash Flow
  cycle of contributions and
    withdrawals, 138–140
Chase Manhattan Bank, 26–28

Closed feedback loops
  general system, 32
  as criteria for effective
    organization, 37
  institutional examples of, 67
  mathematical model of, 92–99
  impact on performance,
    160–163
Cognitive limits
  effect on security analysts'
    recommendations, 43
Comparison of portfolios
  mathematical foundations,
    140–142
  examples of, 157–163, 165,
    170–171
Computer programs
  availability for alternative
    portfolio management
    approaches, 78
  low cost, 172
  See also IAL
Conditional distribution forecasts
  role in structured decision
    making system, 55
  important advantages of, 67
  ability of alternative approaches
    to portfolio management to
    use, 78
Convergence
  of revision algorithms, 115–116
Correlated observations
  mathematical corrections for,
    142–143
Cyert, R. and March, J.
  behavioral analysis framework,
    37–39
  relevance to managers, 175
  relevance to management
    scientists, 177

See also Behavioral flow analysis

D
Data
  conditions for reliability, 7
  factors limiting scope of, 10
  examples of, 56
  sources of, 132
  macro economic conditions
    coincident with, 133–135
Diversification. See Markowitz,
  Prudent Man Doctrine, upper
  bounds

E
Evaluation of Organizations
  criteria, 37–39
  pension funds, 39–43
  alternative structures, 157–163
Evaluation of Security Analysts
  normal practice, 39–43
  using the structured decision
    making system, 53
  examples of, 167–169

F
Feedback correction
  appropriateness for alternative
    portfolio models, 78
  mathematical models of, 92–99
  single stock complications,
    120–122
  effects of, 160–163
  See Closed feedback loops,
    conditional distribution
    forecasts, Theil, H.
First National Bank and Trust
  Company of Chicago, 26–28

G
Goals
  portfolio safety, 99–111, 115–119
  security safety, 119–126
  ignoring risk, 126
  qualitative, 126–128
  random, 128

H
Hypotheses tested, 151–156

I
IAL
  Investment Analysis Language, 172
Index Funds
  motivation for, 18
  estimated fees for management of, 148
  impact on performance, 170–172

M
Macro Economic Forecasts
  as input to portfolio strategy, 54
  results of for simulation tests, 134
Management goals
  non-measurable, 40
  satisficing, 50
  risk-return tradeoff specification, 106
  impact on performance, 157–163
Management process
  total system overview, 8
  simulation of, 129.
  See also Behavioral flow
Management systems
  alternative formulations, 150
  superiority of selected, 157–163
  See also Management process
Market efficiency, 17
  See also Index Funds, Performance measurement
Market funds, *See* Index funds
Market excess return
  moments of, 104–105
  covariance assumptions, 104–105
Market excess return variance
  estimation mathematics, 82–85, 104–105, 109
  impact of feedback correction on performance, 160
Markowitz, H.
  foundations of portfolio theory, 43–44
  definition of risk, 45–47
  illustration of diversification, 65
Mean-variance objective
  normative theory, 43–46
  modified for safety first risk, 106–110
  impact on performance, 159, 162.
  See also Markowitz, H.
Mellon National Bank and Trust Company, 26–28
Mlynarczyk, F.
  analysis of beta instability, 21
Morgan Guarantee Trust, 26–28
Multiperiod considerations, 73–76

O
Operational portfolio
  management models, 71–76
Organizational components
  Leavitt framework, 4, 5

P

PIE models
  role in process, 8
  mathematical formulation of, 31
  use in practice, 33–34
Parameter values
  initial settings, 148–149
  effects of variation in on performance, 156–163
Pension funds
  growth in, 12
  concentration of control, 12–13
  characteristics of management personnel, 15–17
  economic justification for, 17–18
  qualitative definition of return from, 100
  mathematical formulation of expected return from, 102–103
  representative performance of, 164–166.
  See also Management process
Performance
  competitive standards, 164–166
Performance measures
  Treynor's, 20
  Jensen's, 21
  Sharpe's, 21
  BAI recommendations, 22–23
  industry practice, 41
  sensitivity of management evaluation to, 164–165.
  See also Capital market line, Risk
Prudent Man Doctrine
  legal definition of, 14
  claim on bank capital, 14
  conflict with normative theory, 15, 45–49
  impact on diversification practices, 35
  mathematical formuation of, 119–126
  impact on performance, 156

Q

Qualitative goals, 126–128

R

Random selection
  goal formulation, 128
  impact on performance, 158
Recommendations
  portfolio managers, 175–176
  security analysts, 177
  management scientists, 177–179
  corporate management, 179–180
Reports
  conditional forecasts of security prices, 56
  return implications, 57
  Structured Decision Making system portfolio management, 62
  complete system management, 167–168
  security analyst evaluation, 166–168
  portfolio manager evaluation, 167–168
  portfolio composition analysis, 169
Revision of portfolios
  comparison of alternative models, 78
  See also Multiperiod considerations
Risk
  conflict between theory and

practice, 45–50
  comparison of alternative models, 78
  impact of formulation on performance, 157
  impact of return tradeoff on performance, 161–163
  See also Application problems, Beta models, Capital Market Line, Goals, Performance Mseasurement

S
Security Evaluation Models
  traditional practice, 31–34
  failure of mathematical models to be excepted, 50–51
  security excess return estimation mathematics, 85–87
Security excess return variance
  estimation mathematics, 86–87
  impact of feedback correction on performance, 160
Sharpe, W. F.
  portfolio selection model, 78
  portfolio composition analysis, 143–145
  See also Beta models, Performance Measurement
Skewness
  inclusion in forecasts, 89–90
  impact on performance, 161
Stone, B.
  quadratic programming simplification, 106
Subjective forecasting
  mathematical formulation of, 80–87
  impact on random selection, 158
  See also Conditional distribution forecasts

T
Taxes, 76
Theil, H
  prodecure for correction of consistent forecast errors, 92–94
Transaction costs
  comparison of alternative models, 78
  mathematical formulation of, 102
  effects of on portfolio revision, 114–115
  estimates of, 135–136
Triangular distribution
  managerial advantages of, 55
  graphical illustrations of, 58–60
  mathematical formulation of, 85
  impact of the use of on performance, 161.
  See also subjective forecasting

T
Turing's Test, 6, 25

U
Universe for tests
  size of, 72
  variation in, 72
  See also Data
Upper bounds
  mathematical definition of, 106
  impact on performance, 163
  See also Prudent Man Doctrine
Utility function
  conflict between practice and theory, 48–49
  See also Prudent Man Doctrine